CHEAP
Love

LIVING AND LOVING ON LESS

CHEAP
Love

LIVING AND LOVING ON LESS

CARRIE STARR, MA
ERV STARR, PHD

ILLUSTRATIONS BY MIKAYLA STARR

WESTBOW
PRESS
A DIVISION OF THOMAS NELSON

WestBow Press books may be ordered through booksellers or by contacting:

WestBow Press
A Division of Thomas Nelson
1663 Liberty Drive
Bloomington, IN 47403
www.westbowpress.com
1-(866) 928-1240

Because of the dynamic nature of the Internet, any web addresses or links contained in this book may have changed since publication and may no longer be valid. The views expressed in this work are solely those of the author and do not necessarily reflect the views of the publisher, and the publisher hereby disclaims any responsibility for them.

Any people depicted in stock imagery provided by Thinkstock are models, and such images are being used for illustrative purposes only.

Certain stock imagery © Thinkstock.

ISBN: 978-1-4497-1666-0 (sc)
ISBN: 978-1-4497-1667-7 (e)

Library of Congress Control Number: 2011928114

Printed in the United States of America

WestBow Press rev. date: 06/27/2011

Dedication

To our parents,

Carol, Susan and Ervin, who taught us to

save regularly, give generously, and love unconditionally.

Acknowledgements

Thank you to our precious friends and family members who served as readers, editors, marketers, and encouragers along the way. This book would not exist without you.

Readers: Susan Blocker, Krista Bovee, Bethany Rawleigh, Jamarr Myers, Lexi Nesbitt, and Karolin King

Editors: Samantha Monaghan, Jessica Nicastro, Susan Carl, Rebecca Barringer, and Meg Hartman

Secret Agent: Michael McGinnis

Illustrator: Mikayla Starr

Savior: Jesus Christ

Contents

Introduction:
The Missing Link

Eighteen years ago, we spent our honeymoon in a borrowed tent. Ten years later, we celebrated our anniversary on an Alaskan Cruise.

As we relaxed on our private balcony watching dolphins play in the ocean below, we realized we had a unique story to share. We began hurriedly scrawling down our memories and the idea of "Cheap Love" was born. Our vision was to share the link we discovered between making wise financial decisions and enjoying a fulfilling love relationship.

Money is a leading cause of divorce. Many couples disagree about financial matters and it drives them apart. Two lives cannot be intimately shared without a common vision for how to use money. However, when both partners pursue the same financial goals, it can create a powerful bond between them.

What you are about to read is not a magic formula. It is not a guarantee or a quick fix. It is the true story (our story) of a young couple with a common mission. We were both committed to being debt free, living on less, and pursuing generosity. While striving for those shared goals, we found our greatest asset to be each other. Our radical proposal: the use of money can bring you together as a couple instead of tearing you apart.

Chapter One:

New Beginnings

A Blossoming Friendship

*g*rowing up poor has its advantages. My modest financial
beginnings led me to attend the State University of New
York College at Oneonta, an inexpensive state college where
I would meet the perfect man for me. At first, I was disappointed
that I couldn't attend the private Christian college where many of
my youth group friends were headed. It wasn't until the fall of my
sophomore year that I realized God had better plans for me.

When I arrived at the first Campus Ambassadors (CA) Christian
Fellowship meeting of the year, the circle of students contained
many new faces. One in particular stood out to me. He was short,
wearing glasses, and sitting directly across the circle from me. We
each took turns sharing a story from our childhood. This guy wanted
to share two stories. And they were long stories …with lots of details
… shared with enthusiasm. I was intrigued.

When the meeting was over, I immediately walked across the
room to introduce myself. "Hi! I'm Carrie. I enjoyed your stories

tonight. What was your name again?" I remembered it being an old-man name, but it would not stick in my head.

"It's Ervin. But you can call me Erv. Everyone does."

I couldn't decide which was worse. Erv or Ervin. Maybe he goes by a middle name, I thought- or another nickname.

Erv was a junior who had just recommitted his life to his Christian faith. After two years of living the typical college life, including a fraternity and an unhealthy dating relationship, he was looking for a fresh start. Making new friends and growing in his faith were top priorities for him.

Unfortunately, we weren't able to talk for long. I needed to get back to Littell Hall for a Resident Advisors (RA) meeting, and I was already running late. After making my way across campus, I spent the next two hours discussing floor activities and disciplinary procedures.

When I returned to my dorm room, all the girls on my floor bombarded me with questions. They said a short guy in a tie-dyed T-shirt had just left the building. He had stopped at every room on the floor looking for me. They all wanted to know who he was, but no one had caught his name. I didn't know what to tell them. I was not the kind of girl that guys came searching for. It never occurred to me that the guy from Campus Ambassadors with the old man name would walk clear across campus to see me.

The next day, as I sat in the back of my 11 a.m. class, I noticed someone in the front row. I couldn't tell for sure, but I thought it might be Erv. I leaned out into the aisle just a bit so I could see him a little better. It didn't help much. Having forgotten my glasses, the details were fuzzy. I would have to wait until the end of class to get a closer look.

I spent the next hour distracted. When the professor finally ended her in-depth analysis of Old Testament literature, I initiated my plan. I needed to get close enough to tell if it was really him without being too obvious if it wasn't. I had only met this guy once, so I wasn't even entirely sure what he looked like. Did he wear glasses? I couldn't remember. This guy was wearing glasses. As I neared the front of the room, he was talking to another friend of mine from the Christian fellowship group the night before. That cinched it. It was definitely him.

I re-introduced myself, and he said he remembered me. In fact, he had looked for me at my dorm the night before but couldn't find me anywhere. Tie-dye guy mystery solved.

It was lunchtime so we headed to the dining hall together. Since we were both at school on a combination of academic scholarships and government grants for poor kids, eating in the dining hall meant a free lunch for each of us. We enjoyed getting to know each other better over high calorie cafeteria food. I was disappointed when I glanced up at the clock and saw that it was almost time to leave for my next class.

As soon as lunch was over, the questioning began. My friend Rachel ran into us on our way out of the dining hall. I introduced her to Erv and then said goodbye to my new friend. As soon as he was out of sight, she gave me the third degree. "Who is that guy? How do you know him? Is he the one who was looking for you last night? I heard about that! Do you like him? You guys would make a perfect couple. You're the same height. And you have the same skin tone."

I didn't realize that matching height and skin tone made the perfect couple. Apparently this was a winning combination.

I explained that I had just met him and had too little information to determine if I "liked" him. After further interrogation, I was actually happy that I had to get to my next class. I made a mental note to avoid sitting by Rachel at dinner. I didn't want any more questions.

That night, as I was procrastinating instead of doing my homework, my phone rang. It was tie-dye guy. "Are you going to breakfast?" he asked.

"Probably not," I replied. I usually had a piece of fruit or a granola bar on my way to class, allowing me to sleep as late as possible yet not starve.

"Well, John and I are going to breakfast at 7:30 a.m., and we want you to come too."

"Um … sure. Sounds like fun." I was really thinking, "Sounds pretty early." But, it was nice to be invited, and I didn't want to say, "no."

John and Erv were waiting for me in the dining hall lobby the next morning at 7:30 a.m. They were slouched in the semi-comfortable chairs of the dining hall lobby half asleep. I was amused at their lethargy even though it was *their* idea that we meet at this hour. We dragged ourselves up the stairs and ordered our breakfasts. The dining hall was deserted so we had our choice of seats. Once we sat down and started talking, however, all three of us were wide awake. We found ourselves in the midst of a passionate debate. I don't remember the exact topic of conversation, but it was obvious that all three of us had strong opinions. It was refreshing to be so honest. Though it was tense at times, we enjoyed ourselves and respected each other. We decided that we should do this again.

We soon became "the breakfast club," meeting twice a week to share, talk, argue, and pray. We had others from Campus Ambassadors join us along the way making it even more fun. More opinions and input made the conversation richer. The crowd changed from week to week, but Erv, John and I were the constants. We were always there, and we looked forward to it – even at 7:30 in the morning.

In the meantime, Erv and I found ourselves spending more time together. In addition to free campus breakfasts and free campus lunches, we added free campus dinners to our joint schedules. I moved up to the front row by Erv in our "Bible as Literature" class, and we would meet in the park or the library to do our homework together. We went to our Campus Ambassadors meetings on Thursday nights, and he asked to help lead my small group Bible study every Tuesday night. Between classes, meals, CA and church, we were seeing each other almost every day.

On Common Ground

Through these events we found we had a lot in common. We were both passionate about our faith, enjoyed learning, and loved the inexpensive pleasure of the great outdoors. Other than the limited income we earned from our work study jobs on campus, we were broke. Finding creative ways to have cheap fun became a favorite pastime. While our friends went to the movies or bowling, we organized game nights and scavenger hunts. We found ourselves in a little band of like-minded (and empty-walleted) friends who went biking, camping, and canoeing. With shared gas money, borrowed canoes, and patched tents, we all could enjoy an entire weekend of fun without breaking the bank.

Our love of learning set Erv and I out on new adventures together. Our campus fellowship group didn't have a worship leader, and I was just learning to play guitar. We borrowed a couple of guitars from some nice folks at church and started teaching each other how to play. Though it was a little like the blind leading the blind, we enjoyed learning and serving together. My former roommate had also taught me some sign language. We got out the *Joy of Signing* book and started to teach ourselves that as well. It was free, and we enjoyed it. Because we spent way too much time together to pretend we knew what we were doing, we enjoyed laughing at our mistakes. This allowed us to be real with each other.

By the end of the semester, everyone was talking about "us." The interrogation by Rachel after that first lunch back in September was just the beginning. If I had a dollar for every time someone asked me, "What was going on?" between Erv and me, I could have given up my tutoring job at the campus learning center and bought a new car ... or at least a new bicycle. Every girl on my floor was convinced that Erv liked me, and they kept pushing me to talk to him about it. Meanwhile, I was trying to be content with our friendship and not hope for something more. I didn't want to spoil what seemed like a good thing.

Erv was pretty sick of the comments as well. He had his share of friends tell him he should be dating me, but he would always blow them off. There was a girl (or two) back home that he liked, and he wasn't even sure if he was staying at Oneonta State. He was thinking about transferring as soon as the following semester. He was happy to have a good Christian friend in me and that was it.

In a moment of temporary insanity I allowed myself to initiate a "define the relationship" conversation with Erv. I sat nervously on his door room floor while he sat on his bed, caught completely off guard by the topic. He wasted no time making it clear that he didn't have any romantic feelings for me. In fact, he told me point blank, "I will never date you, so you can get that idea out of your head." That was pretty clear. I put the idea out of my head. Or at least I tried to.

We stayed in touch over the long Christmas break, and Erv decided not to transfer. I was relieved, not wanting to give up my new best friend. We both made visits to each other's houses over the holidays and enjoyed getting to know our respective families. Seeing where we both came from continued to strengthen our friendship. We were surprised to learn how similar our backgrounds were.

We'd both grown up in broken homes and lived with single parents. Our houses were modest and our family cars were in need of repair. Yet because of our parents' economic struggles, we'd both been brought up with the values of hard work and careful financial planning. Instead of feeling awkward, we were right at home as we sat on each other's hand–me-down furniture, eating store brand cookies while playing cards with our parents. We didn't mind waiting to use the one bathroom, because we'd both grown up with only one in our homes. And, of course, we both dressed in layers because the heat was turned down at his house and at mine. Nothing about our home lives needed to be explained or apologized for. We each enjoyed having a friend who considered the other "normal."

As we spent time with each other's families, we were reminded of our parents' generosity while growing up. I shared with Erv that when my mom received some unexpected cash, she used it to buy groceries and secretly left them for a struggling friend at the nearby trailer park. Erv shared that his mom used to bag up her kids' outgrown clothes and share them with the less fortunate family next door. In high school, my mom allowed a friend of mine to live in our home for months while her parents' house was under construction. Erv's home was always open to friends and family members who needed a place to stay. As we continued to trade stories back and forth, it was obvious that our parents were characterized by helping others in need. Hearing these stories helped us appreciate our common roots of giving regardless of income.

Since we attended church together regularly, I had noticed that Erv was committed to giving weekly. At first this surprised me since he was always short on cash. I learned that he was committed to give this money, even if it was a small amount. He also gave support each month to a child in Haiti through Compassion International. I admired this generosity and appreciated his understanding of my own convictions regarding giving. For me, donating a portion of my income at church was a joy. Helping young women through the support of a Christian rehabilitation home was also a priority to me. Though some of our friends didn't understand how we could have "extra" money to give away when we didn't have money for CDs or pizza, this was something we respected and admired in each other. It was yet another value we held in common.

The Godfather and a Good Mother

In the spring, our friendship continued to grow. We appointed ourselves the social coordinators of our Campus Ambassadors group and initiated "Girls' Night Out" and "Guys' Night Out." We would plan inexpensive events where the guys watched macho movies or cooked us girls homemade breakfast. The girls would have dance parties or stay up late talking while eating cookie dough. Our friends also launched a Campus Ambassadors Newsletter in which Erv and I had a monthly column called, "Kumkwat and Kiwi's Excellent Adventures." (These were our nicknames acquired at one of our crazy game nights in the fall.) In these articles we'd share the latest news of our biking, hiking, or traveling adventures. Though the content is totally embarrassing to read today, we spent hours laughing uncontrollably while we penned these outrageous stories.

As the semester drew to an end, things started to change. Erv was going home for the summer. I was staying in town to work with the church youth group. We had become the best of friends in every way, and we were already plotting how we'd stay in touch across the miles. In the last weeks of classes, we decided to have a movie marathon night and watch all three installments of *The Godfather* with our friend John. Our good buddy John got tired during the first movie and left us alone in my dorm room for the next six hours. That was a mistake.

I have a high sensitivity to violence, and *The Godfather* movies are full of people being kicked, punched, and shot. Every time someone pulled out a gun or beat someone up, I would cringe and go into hiding. As this process repeated itself, I found myself sitting closer and closer to Erv. When the last movie ended I realized we were uncomfortably close and in the room all alone. After the whole, "I'll never date you," comment, I figured we were safe. That's when he kissed me. I no longer believe anything he says.

The next day Erv apologized for kissing me and asked if we could pretend it didn't happen. I was disappointed but agreed. We didn't want to mess up our perfect friendship. That night he kissed me again. The mixed messages were a little confusing.

Throughout that week we had many awkward conversations about what was happening in our relationship. We came to the mutual conclusion that we were interested in being more than friends, but we feared ruining our unique friendship. We'd both dated other people before and had our hearts broken. Neither of us was interested in signing up for more heartbreak, and we didn't want to risk hurting each other. We didn't know how to proceed (except Erv wanting to keep kissing me, which I told him he had to stop. At least until we figured this out.)

We decided we needed a little outside help with this one. We made an appointment with our campus minister, who was a trusted friend and father figure to both of us. He told us that there was no way to enter a relationship without risk. We couldn't guarantee where our relationship would go. He explained that moving from friendship to romance was part of God's plan for making families. Did we consider each other someone we would want to marry someday? We both thought that was a strong possibility. He then gave us some warnings and guidelines regarding our physical relationship if we were to start dating and agreed to pray with us about our relationship.

Then we had an unexpected conversation with my mom. She called me at my dorm room when Erv happened to be there. I gave her an update on what was going on between us and she asked to speak with Erv. She shared with him her own tragic love story. She had been abandoned by my dad before I was even born. When I was in middle school she became good friends with a man named Al. They played games together, had long talks, and enjoyed each other's company. Over time, they fell in love, and Al asked my mother to marry him. My mom said no because she didn't want to disrupt the lives of my brother and me. We'd never had a father, and she didn't think it was fair to ask us to accept him as our dad. Al was disappointed but understood. He gave my mom space and moved on. Years later when I went off to college, Al came back. Now that my brother and I were grown up and on our own, he wanted to know if my mom had room in her life for him again. They began dating and started planning a future together.

At the beginning of my sophomore year of college, Al got very sick. Al had suffered from depression during the years that he and my mom were separated and didn't take very good care of himself. He didn't see the doctor, and important medical issues went unaddressed. By the time he was reunited with my Mom, the damage to his heart had been too great. He died during my first week of college that year (the same week that I had met Erv). It was a great loss to my mother. She could not help but regret postponing a future with Al. She told Erv that there are no guarantees of the future. If we loved each other, we needed to act now and enjoy one another while we could. She ended her conversation by telling him to, "Go for it!" because today was the only day we had for certain. That night we officially started dating.

Thanks, Mom.

Erv's Bottom Line

- ✖ You can be content with little.
- ✖ There are a number of "fun" things to do for little to no money.
- ✖ Be generous.
- ✖ Friendship is a strong foundation for a long-term relationship.
- ✖ Romance involves risk.
- ✖ Enjoy the wisdom of others.

Chapter Two:

The Dating Game

Singing in the Rain

S o now we were dating. The semester was almost over. In a few days, we would be going our separate ways for three long months. Our timing was terrible.

We had one Saturday left to spend together, and we wanted to make it special. I had been telling Erv about a nearby state park I thought he'd love. It had a beautiful lake with a nice beach and great hiking trails. We packed an elaborate picnic of peanut butter and jelly sandwiches along with snacks confiscated from the dining hall and headed out mid-morning. We became a little nervous, seeing the clouds get thicker and darker while driving to the park. By the time we arrived at the beach, we found ourselves in the midst of an absolute downpour. We sat in the car trying to wait it out, but it was clear that this storm was here to stay.

Fighting off our disappointment, we decided to somehow salvage our last special day together. We climbed into the back of the borrowed 1984 Bronco and set up our picnic. I grabbed an apple in one hand and a banana in the other and started singing, "I like to eat, I like to eat, I like to eat, eat apples and bananas."

I was surprised when Erv joined in on the next verse and started singing, "A lake tae ate, A lake tae ake, A lake tae ate, ate aepples and bananaise!"

The song is very silly, and I was delighted that Erv was willing to sing it with me. As the rain got louder on the roof of the car, our singing got louder. Soon we were screaming the song at the top of our lungs.

"O lote to ote, O lote to ote, O lote to ote, ote opples ond bononos!"

As the song ended, we both cracked up laughing at ourselves. We then proceeded to sing more ridiculous camp songs for the next two hours until the sun finally reappeared. Though it was very different than the day we had planned, it turned out to be the perfect way to end the semester together.

As we said our goodbyes for the summer, we both committed to staying in touch. At this time, we were unaware that the Internet had even been invented, so e-mail was not an option. We didn't have cell phones either. We both became proficient at writing old-fashioned letters. I lived in an apartment with some friends for the summer, and I quickly learned exactly what time the mailman arrived each day. In fact, there were many days when I would meet him at the mailbox. We became friends.

After talking almost daily for an entire school year, it definitely took some time to get used to being apart. The letters were a wonderful opportunity to put into words the new things we were both thinking and feeling. The time apart also forced us to grow as individuals and pursue our separate interests. This was a healthy change for both of us as our lives had become so intertwined. About once a week we would catch up over the phone. We enjoyed hearing about the other's adventures and discoveries. There were also the occasional in-person visits, which were a big deal. I enjoyed getting to know his "at home" friends better, and he would tag along at my youth group events. We both gained new-found appreciation for each others' talents and abilities.

We counted down the days until we were back at school. Erv moved into an apartment off campus with John and some other friends. I moved back on campus and resumed my Resident

Advisor duties. Since many of our friends hadn't seen us since May, they didn't know we had started dating. Last year, we had finally convinced everyone that there was nothing going on between us. Now there was. This was going to be complicated.

The first time we showed up at an event holding hands, everyone stared. It was a little like being in Junior High School. We were so glad when the demands of classes started to increase and everyone finally had homework to do. We were tired of our relationship being the center of people's attention. After we got past all of the annoying, "I told you so," comments, people almost started acting normal around us.

A Day in the Park

There were other challenges to our new-found status of "dating." The word "dating" seems to imply going out somewhere and spending money. In fact, some would argue that in a committed dating relationship this should happen on a fairly regular basis. Being separated over the summer had saved us a lot of money. Our major expenses were postage and the occasional long distance phone call. Now that we were together in person, we were curious how we'd fit going on dates into our budget. The spending money we both had barely covered school-related expenses such as textbooks and testing fees. There wasn't much leftover to be spent frivolously. We would need to enjoy each others' company in ways that were creative and, more importantly, cheap.

Fortunately, our common love for the outdoors kept a world of inexpensive opportunities open to us. Our favorite date destination became the local park. There were actually two parks in our small college town, allowing us a little variety. My favorite place to go was Wilber Park. Not only did it have a great playground and picnic area, it had walking trails that meandered through the woods. I had enjoyed this park almost weekly during my first two years of college. Before meeting Erv, I would escape to the park after a long day of classes. I'd wander through the woods listening to my walkman, forgetting about homework and roommates and tests. I enjoyed bringing Erv to this special place. We'd pack our picnic lunches from the dining hall and enjoy them in the shade of the huge walnut trees. Then we'd hit the trails together and talk about whatever happened to be on our minds that day. Sometimes we'd tell stories from our childhoods. Other days we'd share our dreams for the future. I continued to be intrigued by Erv's openness and valued his honesty, even when we disagreed.

Erv's favorite park was Neawah. This was where the Oneonta Yankees played baseball, and many of their games were free to college students. We enjoyed cheering on the home team while munching on hot dogs and drinking from our water bottles that we filled with tap water. Neawah Park also had great open fields for playing Frisbee or tossing a football. Growing up without a dad, I'd never played catch in the yard like the other kids in my neighborhood. This was a favorite childhood pastime of Erv's, and he was anxious to share it with me. Neawah Park became my sports training camp where I tried my best to keep Erv's boyhood hobby alive. It was a test of his patience and my humility.

The playground in both parks was where we could be the most childlike. We would design elaborate obstacle courses, challenging ourselves to use as many pieces of the equipment as possible. We were especially pleased when we could craft a route where your feet never touched the ground. After we had the passage planned out, we would time each other making our way across the monkey bars and suspension bridges. If the other person's time beat our own, we'd have to make the course more complicated. I'm sure our competitiveness provided some great entertainment for onlookers at the park.

Sometimes the local kids would end up joining us in our little competition. It was on one of these occasions that I saw a different side of Erv. A small boy who seemed about four-years-old slipped off the monkey bars and landed hard on the wood chips below. Before I was fully aware of what had happened, Erv was bent over checking this small stranger for bumps and bruises. He treated the boy with such tenderness and compassion. He dried the little guys' tears with his shirt sleeve and safely returned him to his mommy. In that moment, I got a glimpse of the man I wanted to be my husband. I had thought it before, but this time, I could see it. It was scary and exciting all at the same time.

As the beauty of fall gave way to the chill of winter, we stayed committed to our dates in the park. Bundling up in layers, our boots would crunch along the snow covered paths of Wilber Park. Sometimes we'd build snowmen in the picnic areas or dodge snowballs while running across the fields. The frozen pond at Neawah was open for free skating, and we'd chase each other in circles around the slippery ice. Our most creative winter endeavor was when we retrieved some cardboard boxes out of the recycling room in my dorm. We fashioned them into sleds and proudly took them to the park. Admiring their speed, the neighborhood kids asked to take turns with our cardboard creations. We set new records in our homemade sleds.

Creative and Memorable

Finding inexpensive ways to "date" wasn't our only challenge. Dating also usually involves a certain amount of gift giving. We'd need to find meaningful ways to express our feelings for each other without spending money we didn't have. As the florist was delivering rose bouquets for girls on my floor, Erv was out picking wildflowers by the side of the road. For special occasions, we exchanged our share of greeting cards made from construction paper and magic markers. We also both tried our hand at writing poetry. At the time, our poems seemed very romantic and meaningful. Reading them now is just plain embarrassing!

As Erv's 21st birthday approached, I wanted to do something really special for him. A homemade card or second-rate poem was not going to do. I could think of countless things to buy, but an expensive gift was out of the question. I decided to use all the resources at my disposal and plan a unique experience instead. Waking up at 6 a.m., I grabbed my guitar and walked the two miles between my dorm on campus and Erv's apartment downtown. I woke him up by throwing rocks at his bedroom window. (The sports training at Neawah Park was coming in handy!) I attempted to serenade him from the driveway below and then offered him a breakfast of chocolate croissants that I'd picked up at the nearby bakery. While he was at class later that day, I took tissue paper and streamers and wrapped his car like a giant present. When Erv finally got through the wrapping, his car was filled with balloons and an invitation to dinner. When he arrived at the designated location, I had filled our friend's apartment with tea-light candles and prepared him a delicious meal of homemade sweet and sour pork. Erv was thrilled with his birthday celebration, and I had spent a total of $12.

This same creativity served us well during the holidays. We both had the desire to show love and appreciation to our families at Christmastime. Instead of buying overpriced gifts, we decided to make them. We copied poems and favorite Scripture verses onto ordinary printer paper. Next we very carefully burnt the edges of them attempting to give them a charred aged look. We completely torched a few, but overall we were quite successful. We placed the ones we didn't incinerate into dollar store frames and wrapped them in comics from the Sunday paper (this was the wrapping paper of my childhood). They actually turned out beautifully and everyone loved them.

Probably the most favored of all our homemade Christmas presents were the coupon books entitling our loved ones to household chores, a listening ear, or a big bear hug. We gave these to our parents, siblings, friends, and roommates. Our parents appreciated the household chores when we were home, and our roommates enjoyed making it our turn to clean the toilet! Though we made these in college, Erv's mom recently redeemed one of those coupons for a night out with her son. That gift lasted much longer than anything we could have bought at the mall.

As part of our "dating" experience, we also got into the habit of reading together. We both love books and had several favorites that we wanted to share. We would select a book from the library and then take turns reading chapters aloud to each other. Sometimes we'd take our book to the park and other times we'd just sit in the living room at Erv's apartment. After reading together, we had so much to talk about. We enjoyed discussing the characters and guessing where the plotline was headed next. We also continued to be study buddies and would help each other with our homework. Erv was my math expert, and I was his typist. It was a good arrangement.

A Penny Saved

As our relationship progressed, we found ourselves talking about "The Future." I was unaware of this at the time, but as talk of marriage became a reality, Erv literally began saving his pennies to purchase an engagement ring. I wondered why he never had change on him! I found out later that he was intentionally breaking bills to make more change. He'd go home and put the change into a huge glass jar that he kept hidden in his bedroom closet. When it wasn't adding up fast enough, Erv started saving his one dollar bills as well. After being diligent for the entire year, my intelligent boyfriend started researching quality rings at discount prices. He was determined to pay cash and wanted to get the best ring he could at a price he could afford.

In the meantime, another school year came to an end. Erv was graduating, and I was preparing for my senior year. When I moved off campus into an apartment for the summer, I couldn't find what I had done with my class ring. It wasn't in the box with my other jewelry. I assumed it had been misplaced while rushing to get packed. In the meantime, Erv went on an unexpected trip out of town. I honestly don't remember the excuse he gave me, but with my ring missing, I was a little suspicious. Stealing my ring would have been the perfect way to ensure buying the properly sized engagement ring.

That summer Erv and I worked together with the church youth group. To make sure we were appropriate examples to the teens, we were asked by the church leadership to refrain from acting like a couple around the students. We didn't hold hands or hug or any other "couple-like" things. It was actually fun for us to pretend there was nothing going on between us for a whole summer. We enjoyed the kids we worked with and had a great time being a team. It was a wonderful opportunity to learn how our different strengths as leaders worked together. In fact, by the end of the summer, there were several parents telling us that we would make a great couple. We tried not to laugh out loud at them.

As the summer came to an end, I was getting ready to begin student teaching. My birthday was coming up, and Erv wanted me to go camping with his family in Maine to celebrate. I was torn because my cooperating teacher invited me to help her spend the week before school setting up her classroom. This was a good opportunity for me, and I really felt obligated to do it. Erv was insistent that I find a way to go with him instead. I couldn't help thinking about the missing ring last May and wondered if this was why Erv was being so adamant. I didn't want to miss out on what could be a most memorable engagement birthday, so I worked out a compromise. I would help out at the school for most of the week and then enjoy a long weekend camping.

Arriving the day before my birthday, I was greeted by Erv's entire family. We spent the afternoon enjoying Old Orchard Beach and then the giant water slide at the campground with his younger brothers and sister. I helped his mom and grandmother cook dinner that evening, and later we sat around the campfire playing cards. Erv and I made plans to get up early to watch the sunrise the next morning for my birthday. I was nervous and excited. It sounded like a perfect proposal opportunity, but I did not want to be disappointed. I made myself believe that nothing was going to happen and tried to get some sleep.

The next morning Erv's mom hurriedly woke us up. Apparently whatever alarm we'd set didn't go off, and the sky was already beginning to get light. Frazzled, we quickly jumped into the car. We drove down to the beach and parked in a one-hour tow-away zone. Erv grabbed a brown paper bag and his guitar. I snatched the blanket packed by Erv's mom, and we ran down to the water's edge. As we spread out the blanket, the sun was just starting to come up over the horizon. Our timing was perfect after all.

We sat together quietly enjoying the beautiful reds and golds of the sunlight contrasted against the dark blue sky. It was gorgeous. Several minutes passed before Erv finally broke the silence.

"Do you want your birthday present?"

By now, I was so nervous, I could barely speak. This was rare for me. I nodded my head.

He handed me the brown paper bag. I opened it and tried not to act disappointed.

It was *The Prophet* by Frank Peretti. It was a book we'd wanted to read for a while. I'd been excited about it all summer until that moment. This was not the special present I was hoping for.

"Thanks," I said, trying to be sincere. "We can start reading it today." I hugged the book to my chest and stared out at the ocean. Maybe I should have just stayed back and helped out more at the school. Maybe things weren't going where I thought they were going. I was a fool to get my hopes up. That's when Erv pulled the guitar out of its case.

He started singing a song I had never heard before. As he sang, I realized that it was a song he had written. He sang about our friendship and the many things he valued about me. It was overwhelming. I went from feeling awfully disappointed to feeling very loved and appreciated. That's when I heard a line in the song that I couldn't quite make out. The waves were crashing and the wind was blowing, but I thought I heard him sing, "… and I ask you if you'll marry me?"

That couldn't be what he just said. I didn't want to assume it and be wrong … again. How many times could I be disappointed in one morning?

Then the song ended. Erv put the guitar aside and got down on one knee. This time the message was clear. "Will you marry me?" he asked.

I was so nervous, I didn't know what to say. Of course I wanted to say "Yes!" That would have been the right answer. That's what I meant to say. But that's not what came out of my mouth. I have this terrible habit of making jokes when I'm nervous. Humor is supposed to relieve tension and awkwardness. Even though I was hoping and even somewhat expecting this to happen, I found myself completely unprepared for the awkwardness of the moment.

"I'll think about it," was the humorous reply that came out of my mouth. Erv fell over in the sand. I was not funny.

I quickly regained my senses and told him, "Yes, of course," as I helped him up out of the sand. Being gracious, he forgave my nervous humor. He pulled the simply beautiful quarter-carat diamond ring out of his pocket and put it on my finger.

Wait until the youth group parents hear about this.

Erv's Bottom Line

- ✖ Silly makes good memories.
- ✖ Love means making sunny days out of rain storms.
- ✖ Words (letters, texts, email, cards) mean a great deal.
- ✖ Dating can be cheap (that is: not costly- emotionally or financially).
- ✖ Communication takes time and gives room.
- ✖ Creativity opens endless ways to let others know how much you care for them.
- ✖ A little saved over time adds up to a diamond.

Chapter Three:

The Budget Wedding

Patience and Timing

Now that we were finally engaged, we were anxious to be married. As we began looking at our academic calendars, spring break seemed like a perfect time. I had a week off from college and Erv had a week off from the seminary he was now attending. An April date would allow us eight months to make all of the necessary arrangements. That still seemed like an awfully long time to wait, but a Christmas wedding would not allow us enough time to get everything done. We set our date for April 3rd and began making preparations.

Our parents, who had been very happy for us up until this point, were not pleased with the date. They thought it was too soon. They wanted us to wait until August so I could focus on student teaching and finish my degree before getting married. We found ourselves in the midst of a conflict. Despite the tension it caused, Erv and I decided to tentatively move forward with our April plans. We were grown-ups, and it was time to start making decisions on our own. Hopefully our parents would come around and see it our way.

In the meantime, other issues came to the surface. Now that we were getting married, the temptation of physical intimacy became stronger. We both had a commitment to sexual purity before marriage and had struggled to maintain our mutually agreed upon boundaries while dating. Being engaged only made it more difficult to exercise self-control. After failing to respect our boundaries on multiple occasions, we recognized what we considered to be a serious problem. If we could not trust each other to have self-control before we were married, how could we be sure that we would honor one another and be faithful to each other after we were married? We decided that we needed to maintain absolute purity for a significant amount of time before we would call each other "husband" and "wife." If we could not do that, our relationship could not move forward.

It was at this time that we reconsidered the wisdom of our parents and changed the date to August. Not only did their preferred later date give us the time of purity we felt was essential, it also allowed us to employ many cost-cutting strategies for the wedding. It allowed plenty of time to make our own invitations, favors, decorations and gifts for the wedding party. The extended time also made it possible for us to explore more options for reception halls, photographers, and DJs. As a result, we found an inexpensive fire hall for the reception, I learned that the husband of one of my college classmates was a photographer who was willing to give us a great rate, and Erv's second cousin offered to be our DJ at a significant discount. These discoveries did not come quickly but rather were the result of careful research over time.

In addition to the saved money, an August wedding date meant we could take an extended honeymoon. Erv was now a full-time graduate student in seminary. The program was rigorous and ran 11 months of the year. He had short breaks at Christmas and Easter, but he was off the entire month of August. Since I would be finished with college and awaiting a full-time teaching job to begin in September, we realized we would be free to take a one month honeymoon! With all of these benefits, we wondered why we hadn't listened to our parents' advice sooner. In this one decision we had honored our parents, established greater trust between each other, saved money, and quadruped the length of our honeymoon. This was delayed gratification at its best!

The fall semester passed quickly. Student teaching was rewarding but challenging. I didn't have a vehicle so I had to carpool with a fellow student teacher working in the same building. Most days one of us would need to go in early or stay after late. By the middle of the fall semester, I was leaving for school before dawn and coming home in the dark every day. Sharing a ride did, however, allow both of us to save significantly on gas for the 60 mile round-trip drive each day. Every dime of that savings went into the "wedding fund," along with all of Erv's spare change.

Meanwhile, Erv's graduate work buried him in the study of Hebrew, Greek, and theology. The seminary he attended was located out of state so he had to travel on a weekly basis for classes. He too found carpooling to be an economical solution as he shared a ride with three other seminary students from across New York State. Every week he and his friends would drive six hours to the seminary, sleep on the floor of a local church to avoid paying hotel costs, attend eight hours of classes, and then drive the six hours home. The remaining five days a week were spent reading textbooks, writing papers, fulfilling learning contracts, and volunteering 20 hours a week in ministry. Erv definitely felt the increase in difficulty as he moved from undergraduate to graduate level work.

The sudden change to both of our relaxed schedules added new challenges to our relationship. Our free time was limited so we had to be creative as we looked for ways to spend time together. We were both renting apartments now, and fortunately, we lived only two blocks away from each other. This allowed for spontaneous opportunities to cook dinner for each other or at least stop in for a brief work break. Erv would drop off Elmer's glue to help me with a project I was making or I would walk over just to tell him "goodnight." We would leave encouraging notes on each other's front doors. These served as reminders that even though we didn't see each other much, we were thinking of each other. I decided to volunteer in the same ministry as Erv so we could see each other at least one evening a week. He would occasionally drive me to school just so we could talk in the car. We were glad that this situation was temporary and looked forward to one day living under the same roof.

Humility and Generosity

As the second semester got underway, we discovered just how stressful it is to plan a wedding. It is especially challenging when you are committed to paying cash. Though our parents are very generous people, their resources were limited. With their help and our savings, we had less than $2,000 to spend on our wedding. While looking at prices, we were shocked to discover that we could spend our entire budget on a single purchase! As quotes came in from florists, caterers, and bridal shops, it became obvious that we were not going to have the typical wedding.

We found the biggest expense to be providing food at the reception. This was going to be a problem. We had a guest list of more than 300 people that neither of us was willing to cut in order to reduce our costs. Our friends and family were a high priority, and we didn't want any of the special people in our lives missing this important day. There must be a way to accommodate a large number of people without going into debt. A very unconventional idea came to me that I decided to run by Erv.

"Have you ever been to a pot-luck dinner?" I asked him.

"Yeah. Our family does them all the time," he said.

"Okay good! So you'll know what I'm talking about. Our church always had them growing up. Each family would bring a dish to pass and there was plenty of food for everyone. In fact, there was always food left over. Everyone loved them because you knew you were going to get something you liked. Why couldn't we do that for our reception?"

"Do you think that would really work?" he asked me.

"I think it'd be great. No matter how many people come, there will be enough food for everyone. It will be like an old-fashioned picnic."

"Sounds good to me." Erv said. "You take care of the details and just tell me when and where to show up. I'll be planning the honeymoon."

I was getting pretty used to hearing this line. I began to wonder why I even asked his opinion.

I was so excited about this idea, I got right to work. Because we were renting a fire hall, we were welcome to bring our own food. This was a huge advantage over other reception locations that required you to use their catering service. Erv's large extended family graciously offered to cook extra food to ensure there'd be enough for out of town guests. Erv's aunt volunteered to make our wedding cake as her gift to us. Both of our moms started picking up extra bottles of soda every time they went to the grocery store, and I began stocking up on paper products whenever they went on sale. As the invitations went out requesting people bring a dish to pass, we received many encouraging comments about how weddings used to be done this way. Our guests were enthusiastic about our reception that was reminiscent of days gone by. We were excited to know we could accommodate the 230 guests that replied "yes!" to our invitations.

This out-of-the box idea got us thinking about other typical wedding expenses. Since all of my bridesmaids were poor college students and struggling recent graduates, we decided to buy material and sew the bridesmaids' dresses ourselves. My friend Meg spent countless hours creating the finished products. As I looked at options for my own dress, the price tags made my head spin. Though I was hesitant, we pulled my mother's wedding dress out of her back-room closet. It was a perfect fit! And it was so much prettier than it looked in the pictures I had seen growing up. After a trip to the dry cleaners, the dress was like new. I now had a beautiful wedding gown that meant so much more --and cost so much less -- than anything I could have bought at the store.

While I was busy with wedding details, Erv was true to his word planning the honeymoon. We both love camping and traveling, so we decided we would spend our first month of marriage on a cross-country road trip. Growing up on the east coast, neither of us had spent much time down south or out west. Erv crafted a route that would take us through as many states and national parks as possible during our four-week time frame. We would take the southern route out and the northern route back. Our big destination would be the Grand Canyon, a place we'd both always dreamed of going. With Erv's 1984 Ford Tempo in need of serious repair, Erv's grandparents offered to loan us their more reliable Subaru to increase the odds of us making the trip safely.

We started making an inventory of our camping supplies for the big adventure and realized that we were missing many key items for our cross-country survival. Fortunately, we made this discovery as we were registering for shower and wedding gifts. As friends and family members ventured out shopping, they did not find china patterns or sterling silver on our gift registry. They were surprised to find camp stoves, lanterns, sleeping bags and coolers instead. We knew we wanted camping to be part of the Starr family lifestyle, and these items would serve us better than fancy dishes reserved for special occasions. This also allowed us to save significantly on our honeymoon since these supplies ensured we would not need to pay for hotels or restaurants on our cross-country trek.

The school year finally came to a close, and I celebrated my college graduation. Erv and I were experiencing significant success in our pursuit of purity. (Both of us living in small apartments in which we shared bedrooms with other people was a big help in this area.) After graduation, I moved into a spare room at our campus minister's house where I was blessed with reduced rent in exchange for child-care and household chores. Leaving my apartment allowed me to put more cash away toward our growing wedding expenses. It also provided the maximum accountability for our physical relationship. Living in a house with four children and a campus minister significantly decreases the opportunities to fool around. At this rate, we could get married knowing we had spent a year honoring each other with self-control and mutual respect.

As our wedding day drew closer, we were humbled at the amount of help we had received to make this upcoming event a reality. The list of people we needed to thank on our ceremony programs got longer and longer. One friend offered to video tape the wedding and reception. Another set of friends wrote a song they would perform at the ceremony. My girlfriends helped me make centerpieces, my future sister-in-law made party favors, and another friend helped turn all of our pictures into slides for a slide show at the reception. Both of our families threw us bridal showers, and our friends hosted a third shower in our college town. It was humbling to be on the receiving end of so much generosity.

The night before the wedding, our friends and family continued to bless us with their hard work and helpfulness. We spent hours at the fire hall blowing up balloons, hanging streamers, and setting up tables. Putting out place settings for 230 guests is a time consuming task! As we set the chafing dishes out on the empty food tables, we were humbled at the thought that our guests would be providing our wedding feast. Once the reception hall preparations were finally complete, we attended our rehearsal and rehearsal dinner. In addition to all the food they were preparing for the coming day, Erv's family also cooked all of the food for our rehearsal dinner. With a wedding party of 16 people, it was a generous gift. When the food was gone, it was time for the guys and girls to go their separate ways. I said goodnight to my fiancé for the last time.

Going to the Chapel

It was 2 a.m., and I couldn't sleep. I was too excited. I tossed and turned. By 5am I gave up on sleeping. I headed outside and went for a walk. The sun slowly started to light up the early morning sky. "It's finally here," I thought. Our wedding day begins. With my friends still sound asleep, I grabbed a blanket and spread it out on the lawn. I laid in the sunshine for at least an hour, thinking, praying, and reading my Bible. It was already warm on this first day of August. The sky was clear and beautiful. Today was going to change everything. I soaked in my last few moments of complete independence and solitude, then slowly gathered my things and headed toward my future.

My friends and I spent the morning picking purple heather and Queen Anne's lace in the fields near Erv's grandparents' house. We arranged them in mason jars and decorated the church and reception hall with our homemade bouquets. They rivaled any florist creations we could have purchased. Meanwhile, Erv and his friends busied themselves painting directional signs and posting them along the country roads so that none of our guests would be lost on their way to the ceremony. Though it was tempting to both of us, we avoided seeing each other as we criss-crossed our way around the small town with our last minute errands.

The church where we were getting married had a small, detached building that served as a meeting hall. We had claimed this spot as my dressing room. My bridesmaids showed up in their beautiful flowered dresses, but I arrived in my red plaid bathrobe. I delayed putting on Mom's wedding gown, not wanting the fragile fabric to get wrinkled or stained. We snuck around to the back door to avoid being seen by my guests. It was locked. My mom checked the front door. It was locked too. Confusion erupted amidst the wedding party as we all tried to determine who had the key. As the minutes ticked by and the key was yet undiscovered, I got very nervous. As the hour of our wedding got closer and closer, the parking lot got busier and busier. I did not want to march through a crowd of arriving guests in my bathrobe to change in the church rest room.

It was now five minutes before 3 p.m. and I was desperate. I do not like being late. I certainly didn't want to be late for my own wedding. As we stood in the backyard of the church meeting hall, I surveyed the landscape. Taking inventory of the distance to the nearest road, the few houses facing the yard, and the tall trees scattered around the perimeter, I determined my current spot of grass would serve well enough as my changing room. I wished for a bush or some shrubs to hide behind, but there weren't any. I decided to create a human barrier instead. I had my bridesmaids, my mother, my aunt and a cousin circle up around me as I dropped my bathrobe and struggled to quickly slip the wedding gown over my head. Since everyone I knew in the world was out of view in the parking lot or seated in the church for my wedding, I comforted myself with the thought that if anyone had seen me, I had only exposed myself to complete strangers. Just as my mother was pulling up the zipper, our pastor came around the corner with the missing key.

Now that I was fully dressed and looked like a bride instead of a hospital patient, we all scurried across the parking lot just in time for the mothers to be seated. I had almost caught my breath by the time "Canon in D" started playing. It was my turn to walk down the aisle. As my brother and I stepped through the double doors, I was overwhelmed by the crowd that stood before me. The church was full of all the special people I had known throughout my lifetime. While we slowly made our way down the aisle, I looked into the eyes of so many people that I loved. These were individuals who had supported me, encouraged me, and cared for me as I had grown from a little girl into a young woman. Then, as I looked straight ahead, I met the eyes of the man who would soon promise to support, encourage, and care for me for the rest of my life. This was the moment I had been waiting for.

As we approached the altar, I took Erv's hand. Our pastor prayed and then shared about the meaning and commitment of marriage. He challenged us that marriage was going to require more from us than any relationship ever had in the past. We would need to be willing to serve, sacrifice, and forgive each other on a daily basis and it would take incredible resolve to make it work. We had heard this for weeks before in our pre-marital counseling. In fact, our pastor had told us in one of our sessions that most people would not get married if they knew in advance how much work it would really be. He believed the fact that "love is blind" was actually a great blessing that kept us moving forward toward the impossible.

When our pastor ended his sermon on the joys and challenges of marriage he then transitioned into the sharing of vows. He looked first at Erv and asked, "Will you take this woman to be your wedded wife; to love and to cherish, in sickness and in health, for better or for worse, until death do you part?" This question can be confusing. Not only is it the most grandiose promise in all the world, but practically speaking, there is controversy over how this question should be answered. Since you are asked, "Will you …?" the grammatically correct response would be, "I will." However, when you watch movies or TV shows, the bride and groom usually say, "I do." Because I tend to over-think things, I had gone back and forth about which I would say. I was thankful that Erv was going first. I decided to say whatever he said so we would match. Apparently, Erv had given his response some thought as well. As the pastor finished his question, Erv responded in a loud, clear voice for all two hundred and thirty guests to hear, "I most definitely do!"

I was overwhelmed by Erv's enthusiastic response. I was also at a complete loss as to what I would say on my turn. I certainly could not respond the same as Erv. His response was perfect. It was a classy move that made me feel so loved. How could I simply say "I do" or "I will" after that? I tried to think of something quickly. As demonstrated by my response to Erv's proposal, I am not charming under pressure. This was my wedding day. Surely I could come up with something expressing that I loved him as much as he loved me.

The pastor now looked at me and asked, "Will you take this man to be your wedded husband; to love and to cherish, in sickness and in health, for better or for worse, until death do you part?"

I responded, "Absolutely!"

It was the best I could come up with under pressure.

Charming as we both sounded, neither of us had a clue what we were saying.

Erv's Bottom Line

- ✖ A wedding is step one in a life long journey together. Don't step off the cliff edge by going into debt for one day's celebration.
- ✖ Spend what you have, not what you don't.
- ✖ People who love you will give generously; it takes a village to have a wedding.
- ✖ Simple is beautiful.
- ✖ Nature provides free resources – flowers, beautiful backgrounds, and scenery.
- ✖ When you cut the cake, don't smash it in each others' faces. Honor your new spouse.
- ✖ Marry your best friend.
- ✖ If you can't live with the person as they are today, you won't want them tomorrow since you're not likely to change them.

Chapter Four:

The Camping Honeymoon

Little Cabin in the Woods

We left the reception hall in a silver 1988 Reliant K car. It was a generous wedding gift from Erv's grandparents. The fact that this car was less than a decade old made it feel showroom new to us. We splurged that first night by staying at a lovely bed and breakfast just down the road from our fire hall reception. A charming 1860 farmhouse was the perfect place to begin our new life together. The cheery, elderly proprietors peeked blushingly around the corner as Erv picked me up and carried me across the threshold of our honeymoon suite. This romantic moment ended quickly as we then ran out to the car three more times to bring in our luggage and assorted wedding gifts.

Once we had unloaded all of the loot, we changed out of our wedding clothes into comfy shorts and t-shirts. Now, for most couples who have been waiting to have sex until they are married, they might have other things on their mind. We are not your normal couple. The first thing we did as husband and wife was open all of our wedding cards and count our money. This was important since we had no money for the honeymoon. None. We had budgeted for the B&B that night, but the fate of the remainder of the month laid in that stack of Hallmark cards piled high in front of us. We opened and read each one, blessed by the encouraging words and advice given by our loved ones. As we opened each card, I collected the checks and Erv collected the cash. We honestly had low expectations since everyone had already given us so much to make the wedding a success. Once the last card was opened, we began counting our individual stacks and then added them together. We could not believe the total. This was more money than either of us had ever seen at one time. The month-long honeymoon was on!

In the morning, we headed off for a week in New Hampshire at my cousins' cabin. The lakeside retreat offered quiet walks, refreshing canoe rides, and lots of quality alone time. In addition to staying in a cabin for free, we saved money by cooking our own meals rather than dining out. This was a fun adventure for us since we hadn't done much cooking together. We enjoyed going to the nearby grocery store and picking out our menu ingredients. It served as a fun challenge for us to see how much food we could get for less than $20. We'd bring our treasures home and make them into award winning meals. Or at least we tried not to burn down the cabin. We soon discovered that neither of us had much experience cooking real food. Ramen noodles and mac and cheese are great for college, but they are not exactly honeymoon cuisine. But by the end of the week, we had both improved, enjoying some pretty tasty meals. And we only set off the smoke alarm twice.

We also discovered lots of cheap entertainment. We share a love for board games and had several Risk marathons. One morning, we started an intense match that lasted until dinnertime. There's nothing like world domination to bring romance into your new marriage. We also watched rented movies and spied on each other in the rustic outdoor shower. There was a zip-line outside, where we'd race to the lake's edge and plunge into the cool refreshing water. We'd hike nearby mountains and explore the far edges of the lake by canoe. Inexpensive as it was, it was a very pleasant first week of marriage!

Rocky Road Trip

Upon the conclusion of our time in New Hampshire, we loaded up our camping equipment and headed south. Little did we know that our frugality would not only give us a honeymoon we could afford, but one that would lay a strong foundation for our marriage. Traveling eight to 14 hours a day by car provided wonderful opportunities for us to work on our communication. In the quintessential genre of a college road trip, we found ourselves trapped in a confined space that forced us to work through our difficulties. This is where we discovered one of our greatest marital challenges.

Reading a map.

A map is essential to a successful road trip. We had a good map. In fact, we had a few good maps. We also had a trip planner from AAA outlining our journey road by road, turn by turn. This, however, is only helpful if you stick to the planned route. Maybe this is our real problem. We both like to be spontaneous.

We blissfully began our journey in New York State, heading south through the Blue Ridge Mountains, and later found ourselves near Hot Springs, Arkansas. While our planned route did not take us directly to Hot Springs, we thought it would be a really neat place to experience. We ventured off course about an hour and drove into the town of Hot Springs. This was our first mistake. We were greeted with big red, white, and blue banners declaring, "Boyhood Town of Bill Clinton," (The president at the time). This was great, but how about signs that said, "The Actual Hot Springs are This Way?" We never found those. In fact, after two hours of asking for directions, wandering around aimlessly, and asking for directions again, we became convinced that there was not a single person in Hot Springs, Arkansas who actually knew where the Hot Springs were. We seriously doubt to this day that they even exist.

Now that we had wasted three hours of our day looking for the hot springs, we decided to cut our losses and get back on the road. We could drive the hour back to the interstate and would still make it to our next campsite by sundown. That was our plan. However, something strange happened as we drove back to the highway. What should have taken only an hour was taking two hours, then three hours. I had somehow misread the route back and took us far off course. Erv was angry, and I felt miserable. The car was silent. For a very long time.

Being trapped in a car with an angry person is not fun. In fact, it is one of the worst kinds of torture a person can experience. You cannot walk away. You cannot run and hide. A shouting match will only get you in an accident. The only option is silence. As previously mentioned, I am not good at being silent. And typically, Erv is not either. Long conversations of endless chatter are characteristically strengths of our relationship. But when miles off course searching for an obscure campsite in the dark, Erv and I were very good at silence.

Fortunately for us, a good night's sleep fixes everything. In fact, just being horizontal together makes for quick improvement. Even though we had been married less than two weeks, we had already become accustomed to falling asleep in each other's arms. The thought of sleeping on the cold, hard ground with a chasm of silence between us was not appealing. By the time we were snuggled into our sleeping bags, we were laughing and teasing each other that, one day, we could brag to the world that we had been to the boyhood town of Bill Clinton. All our friends would be totally jealous.

The next few days went by pretty smoothly. We crossed the Mississippi River, traveled across Texas, and headed into the beautiful southwest. Most of our traveling was done quite inexpensively since we primarily stayed in state campgrounds costing between $10 and $12 a night. We bought groceries along the way and cooked our own meals on our camp stove. It was a real treat when it rained because that meant we had to eat out! (Okay, we didn't have to, but we decided we would allow ourselves that simple pleasure as opposed to cooking in the rain.) The all-you-can-eat breakfast buffet at Shoney's was a glorious sight to behold after days of instant oatmeal and Tang. We continued to keep a close eye on the budget, committed to spending only what we could afford in cash.

Our next big obstacle waited for us at Red Rock Canyon. The official park campsite was only $5. What a bargain! We were so excited to be saving $6 that we quickly pulled into the beautiful canyon campground. We found our site, a small square of dirt surrounded by several other small squares of dirt with tents on them. There was no shade whatsoever. We spread out our tent just as the wind picked up. It blew our tent like a sail, and it almost ripped right out of our hands. I tried to hold it steady while Erv tried pounding in the tent stakes. The ground was as hard as a rock. In fact, the ground was rock. Red rock. It was impenetrable. Erv tried and tried to pound in those stakes. In the meantime, I only have two arms. While I would hold down two corners of the tent, the other half of the tent would blow wildly in the wind. Erv got more and more frustrated as the blowing tent flapped in his face while the red rock ground refused to succumb to his pounding.

I do not get angry very easily. While I found our situation challenging, it did not make me particularly angry. If anything, our sail of a tent was slightly amusing. I tried to keep things laid back and easy going. Everyone else had their tents up around us. Surely there was a way we could succeed. It was only a matter of time. Meanwhile, Erv became so angry that, screaming, he picked the flying tent up over his head, ready to send it crashing into the enormous rock walls of Red Rock Canyon. It was at this moment that I yelled over the roaring wind, "It's not our tent!" This little reminder seemed to bring him back to his senses. We had borrowed this tent from our campus minister and assured him that we would bring it back safely.

Once Erv calmed down, I pointed out that we could put our bags inside the tent. That would keep it from blowing away while we managed to secure it to the ground. We were both amused that this obvious solution hadn't occurred to us earlier. For the record, next time we go to Red Rock Canyon, we will pay the extra six bucks for a better campsite. Perhaps one with grass. And dirt.

Cheating Death and Debt

Both Erv and I had always thought it would be awesome to camp in the Grand Canyon. We inquired about this when we finally arrived at the Grand Canyon park office a few days later. We learned that you need to make reservations well in advance to do this. We were only going to be there for three days. That was not "advanced" enough to help us. Meanwhile, Erv was determined to at least see the Colorado River up close and personal. We asked about taking a donkey ride down and back. This was very expensive and way outside of our budget. While it was tempting to say, "This is a once in a lifetime experience. Let's just charge it and pay it off later," we would not compromise our commitment to the honeymoon we could afford with the cash we had.

We decided to take a short, exploratory hike down into the canyon to check out the more affordable option- hiking by foot. We knew it would be tiring, but the price was right. Free! We passed several signs stating in big bold letters that you should not attempt to hike to the river and back in one day. They listed the number of people who had to be airlifted out and those who had died of dehydration. It sounded pretty serious to me. My new husband was (and still is) not good at following directions. When you tell him not to do something, it's like asking him to please, please do it.

Later that day, while enjoying a hike along the rim of the canyon (a perfectly safe and beautiful way to experience the canyon, in my opinion), we passed a father and his grown sons. They were talking about having hiked to the river and back the day before. Not at all embarrassed at having eavesdropped on their conversation, Erv proceeded to ask them what time they left, how much food and water they took with them, and how long the journey had taken them. Before I knew it, we were getting up the next morning at 6 a.m. to tempt fate.

The trip down was pretty easy. It was actually a lot of fun. We practically ran down to stay ahead of the donkey tours and their donkey droppings. We stopped and refilled our canteens at the two planned water stops along the way. By 10 a.m., we were at the Colorado River. We had accomplished our goal, and Erv was victorious. The river was much colder than we expected and the current was swift. Our images of playing in the water together quickly disappeared since we could not safely go in past our knees. Then we encountered our first sign of real trouble. The canteens were just about empty, and we had no way to filter the water in the river for drinking. The first water stop on the way up was three miles away. No big deal, we thought. We can go three miles without much water.

By the time we packed up our bags and left the river, it was 11 a.m. We started the long, steep climb out of the canyon. Switchback after switchback, the desert sun beat down on us, covering us both with sweat. By noon it was more than 100 degrees, and I was begging Erv for water. We had so little left that he started rationing it. He would count to five as I drank and then pull the canteen away. He stopped drinking completely to make sure there would be enough for me. By 1 p.m, we still were not at the water stop, and I was sure we would never make it out of this God-forsaken canyon alive. I could see myself pictured on the big warning posters. I'm going to die in the Grand Canyon on my honeymoon. It was a pitiful thought. With his hand on the small of my back, Erv started pushing me up the steep canyon path as I had lost the will to move forward.

As the temperature continued to climb, we ran out of water completely. Erv had done his best to make it last, but it was impossible. I started to worry about him as he had stopped drinking long before I had. The path began to level out, and we found ourselves entering "The Indian Garden" section of the canyon. This plateau is covered with beautiful varieties of cactus. It's the only patch of green standing in stark contrast to the red and brown rock all around you. More importantly, this is the location of the water stop. We had finally made it. There were dozens of people there, hot, tired and thirsty like us, waiting for their turn at the single water spigot. When we finally filled our canteens, that water was the most refreshing drink on earth.

It was another three miles of climbing out of the next section of canyon. At least this time we were starting with full canteens. Erv continued rationing so we would not run out before the next water stop. The heat did not let up, and the switchbacks stretched out endlessly before us. Why were we doing this again? Erv and I had climbed several mountains together and had never experienced this. Mentally, it was a completely different strategy. When you climb a mountain, you do your hard work first, reach your destination, and enjoy the easy descent. The canyon was the opposite. We had all our fun in the beginning, enjoyed our reward, and then began the hard work climbing out.

This challenging experience reminded us of our commitment against debt. Going into debt is like climbing to the bottom of the

Grand Canyon. You have all of the fun in the beginning, you reach your desired goal, and then you begin the surprisingly hard work of paying it off ... with interest (which is kind of like climbing in the heat while running out of water). We had decided as a married couple that we wanted our financial lives to be more like climbing a mountain. We would do the hard work and make sacrifices in the beginning so that later we could achieve our goals and enjoy life without the heavy burden of debt.

We reached the second water stop and rested a short while before the final ascent to the rim. By now it was mid afternoon. We were in danger of being in the canyon after dark. Erv and I were determined to make it out in the light. We were also getting hungry, having run out of food.

My favorite food is ice cream. I believe the world would be a happier place if everyone ate ice cream every day. My new husband was well aware of my obsession and used this little fact to motivate me. If we got back to the canyon ridge by 5 p.m., he would buy me ice cream. It was 3:30 p.m., and we were both completely exhausted. On a good day, three miles of uphill climbing could be accomplished easily. On a 100 degree day after hours of grueling climbing, I was skeptical, but determined. The promise of ice cream somehow gave me a second wind, and now I was climbing ahead of Erv, encouraging him to keep up with me. As we neared the top, he was really dragging. "You're not going to make me miss ice cream, buddy," I called back to him. I made it to the top with five minutes to spare.

By the time we got back to the campground, I did not want any ice cream. We were both feeling very nauseous. We laid spread out on our picnic table completely miserable. First Erv threw up. Then I threw up. What had we done to ourselves? Erv started moaning about how this reminded him of his hangover days back with the fraternity. Suddenly his intellectual mind kicked in. "You get sick with a hangover because you're dehydrated. We need to drink water. Lots of it." Since alcohol holds very little appeal for me, I had never experienced a hangover. I thought Erv was crazy. The last thing I wanted to do was eat or drink anything. Insistent that he was right, Erv filled the canteens, and we drank and drank and drank. Erv made me drink so much I thought I was going to float away. It was the complete opposite of when he rationed it on the canyon trail. Now he was forcing it on me.

An hour later, we both felt completely better. Apparently, Erv's drinking fraternity days were good for something. We then ate ice cream for dinner.

From the Grand Canyon, we journeyed on to Zion National Park, the Grand Tetons, Yellowstone National Park, and Mt. Rushmore. We continued shopping for groceries, inexpensive campgrounds, and cheap fun. We climbed rocks, swam in streams, and played catch along the side of the road. We avoided all attractions that required an entrance fee. As we drove, we passed the time reading from "The Hobbit" and the "Lord of the Rings." We sang along with the radio, and I became a fan of country music completely against my will.

The last night, we couldn't find an inexpensive campground, so we slept in our car. All in all, our fantastic four-week honeymoon cost us less than $1,000.

Erv's Bottom Line

- An old car paid for is better than a new car payment.
- Home cooked food costs less every time.
- Sometimes looking is more fun than finding.
- When you can't run, you work things out.
- Don't let the sun go down on your anger.
- When you can afford it, enjoy it.
- A good marriage takes perseverance. You can't give up when the ground is hard.
- Sometimes the solutions are simple.
- If you have a will, there is a way.
- It's a long climb out of debt.
- Crazy sacrifices today make for great stories tomorrow.

Chapter Five:

Newlyweds

The Gift of Cash

Thanks to camping rather than hotels, and cooking on our camp stove rather than dining out, we returned home from our four-week excursion with wedding money to spare. With so many generous guests at our wedding, we literally had thousands left over. How would we spend it?

Our friends have spent their wedding money in various ways. Some of them have used it to pay off the wedding itself or to pay for the honeymoon. Others have bought furniture for their new home. One couple even bought a used car with their wedding money. While all of this sounds lovely, we chose to do something much different. We paid off our school loans. And we paid our car insurance for a year. It wasn't very glamorous, but starting our life together with absolutely no debt was a freeing feeling that greatly blessed our marriage.

This led us to an important foundational discussion as a new couple. It was time to establish a budget. This was going to be difficult. The teaching job I had hoped to get never materialized. I entered the market along with a surplus of newly educated teachers.

There were more than 200 applicants for each job available. Even though I had excellent references and a passion for teaching, I didn't have experience or a master's degree. Schools were looking for someone with both. This left me with the option of substitute teaching, an unpredictable source of income.

Erv was a full-time graduate student. He was willing to work but needed to find something that would accommodate him being out of town part of the week. He also wanted to find something in youth ministry. That's when the church approached us with a plan that was an amazing answer to prayer.

After working as summer youth interns in the past, our church was interested in hiring us to serve as youth pastors for one full year. We could both work part-time and together we would collect a full-time salary. The job was going to greatly help our financial situation. With a predictable income from the church, we made up a monthly budget according to our modest youth pastor salary. Any additional income from my substitute teaching would go directly into savings. We would not count on it for monthly expenses.

We calculated rent, utilities, groceries, car expenses, giving, and entertainment into our budget. We wrote these category names on envelopes and put the allotted amount into the envelopes each month. When the envelope was empty, we would have to stop spending money in that category. Since most of these expenses were fixed, the only ones with flexibility were food, gas, and entertainment. Because we only had one car, I carpooled to substitute teach, and Erv still carpooled to seminary. Having just one car for the two of us kept our auto expenses low (insurance, gas, and maintenance). We continued our challenge of spending just $20 a week on groceries. (This basically meant we ate PB&J and pasta on a daily basis.) And fortunately, we had become accustomed to cheap dates, so it wasn't too difficult to keep entertainment low. Trips to the park and reading books together at the Laundromat became staples in our weekly routine. We also learned the pleasure of discounted matinee movies and "in-dates."

After a while, the envelope system became cumbersome. Once we were pretty well trained as to our financial limits, we switched to keeping track of expenses by category on a piece of paper. There would be a column for each category, and we would subtract from the total whenever we spent money. (This piece of paper would one-day become an Excel spreadsheet.) We kept track of everything from donations at church to milkshakes at McDonalds. When the budget was looking tight, we could look back at our written record and find out exactly where we were overspending. Keeping track of expenses kept us both openly communicating about our wants and needs when it came to money. When we disagreed about a purchase, we had the common ground of our budget to stand on. It saved us from typical marriage arguments about money.

Aunt Linda's Attic

Since we had decided to not spend our wedding money on new furniture, we had some creative problems to solve. We were blessed with a beautiful three bedroom apartment discovered by a real estate agent at our church. The owners of the apartment just happened to be the grandparents of my freshman roommate. We enjoyed very low rent and a generous amount of space. This space was quite empty since we had sparse furniture to fill it. I contributed a used couch and chair from my old apartment. My housemate and I had bought it for $50 out of someone's barn. Erv had his twin bed, which we put in the guest room. My mom let me take my dresser from home for our bedroom. And that was it. We had no place to sleep, eat, or study.

When I was home picking up my dresser, my mom mentioned calling my Aunt Linda. She thought my aunt might have some old furniture she'd be willing to part with. Happy to help, my Aunt Linda guided us through her tour of cast-off furniture. A few hours later we left with a kitchen table, desk, and a dining room table with chairs. We were barely going to have room for it all in our borrowed pick-up truck!

This still left us without a place to sleep. While a twin bed is cozy for a couple of newlyweds, we did not think this was a good long-term solution. After generously giving us a car, Erv's grandparents surprised us with their new queen-sized bed. They had another they could use and wanted us to have this one. Again, we were humbled at the sacrifices others made on our behalf. Our apartment was now complete.

Marriage on a Mission

We had another important decision to make as a newly married couple. We wanted to establish a family mission statement. With Erv having an undergraduate degree in business and both of us being trained in ministry, we knew the importance of mission. If you aim at nothing, you'll hit it every time. We wanted to move forward as a couple and as a new family with a sense of purpose and intentionality. We believed that putting our purpose on paper would guide us toward our shared goals and vision.

After talking for several hours about our hopes and dreams as a couple, we came up with the following statement for the new Starr Family. Here is our statement composed in 1993. Warning: it's long.

"As a family we commit to work as a team, demonstrating in our relationship with each other and those around us the character of Christ by encouraging, sharpening, teaching, learning, listening to, and loving one another. To help meet the needs of those we encounter to the best of our ability.

To live focused on today, with the recognition that this moment may be all we have-before the time we are called to give an account to our Lord and Savior Jesus Christ. To be ready at all times to share and live the message of Jesus. To share all that we have been given and to be good stewards.

To serve and minister to students. To raise our children to be leaders who strive to be like Jesus. To laugh often and keep a positive, hopeful outlook. To cry with those who cry and are hurting. To be open and honest with each other and God. To provide a safe place for those in need. To strive always to know God, each other, and the world in which we minster better. To remain debt free. To conquer fears and to seek justice and truth."

Our mission guided both our time and our money. Just as the budget gave us common ground from which we could make decisions, so did our mission. This was important as we soon learned that there would always be pressing demands that challenge our priorities.

The substitute teaching picked up quickly, and within weeks, I was asked to teach every day. I was hired for maternity leave after maternity leave, keeping me busy from 6 a.m. to 6 p.m. daily. We had weekly prayer meetings and outreach events with the youth group. We also taught Sunday school, planned retreats, and hosted parent meetings. We saw the need to establish a weekly "date night" so our relationship with each other wouldn't get lost in the commotion of united busyness.

Because of our limited budget, we tried to capitalize on creativity instead of cash to enjoy a variety of "in-dates." We played lots of cards (especially pinochle) and board games received as wedding gifts. We also enjoyed candlelight dinners and backyard picnics. These were especially romantic when I managed not to burn our meal. (I was still learning how to cook real food.) Our best "in-dates" came on the nights when Erv would return home after being gone at seminary for a few days. I always planned a special homecoming. I would put signs up around the house, cook a special dessert, or have his favorite music playing. The best homecoming was when I left him clues for a scavenger hunt. I waited patiently hidden in our bedroom closet while Erv made his way around the house searching for the next clue. When he finally found me, we didn't need television or even board games to keep us entertained. Scavenger hunts became Erv's favorite way to be welcomed home.

The Five Year Plan

With weekly "reunions" and no television for the whole first year of our marriage, birth control became an important consideration. Our discussions about birth control actually began long before we got married. Erv and I were both interested in someday having children. In fact, we wanted a whole bunch of children. But we both agreed that it would be best if we waited. First, we wanted to save some money and buy a house. If we saved all of my income and lived only on Erv's salary, it would take about five years to buy a modest house for cash. After talking with a few trusted families from church, we decided that natural family planning was our preferred method to postpone having children.

This particular method of birth control was new to us. Our friends gave us a book that explained in detail what we needed to do. Basically, we would learn when I was ovulating during each month and abstain from sex during that time. It seemed simple and straightforward.

The best part of natural family planning is that it is completely and totally free. There are no purchases to be made, prescriptions to be refilled, or procedures to be paid for. The difficult part of natural family planning is that it requires self-control. To successfully employ NFP, you must be well disciplined and have good communication as a couple. After our year of purity and three years of friendship, we'd gotten pretty good at both. We found NFP to be a very effective method of birth control- as long as we stuck to the plan.

Did I mention that Erv and I both like to be spontaneous?

For our first year of marriage, NFP worked very well. We kept careful track of the days we could enjoy each other and the days we were likely to get pregnant. This became a routine we were both familiar with as we'd romantically ask one another, "Are we in a safe zone," before we'd allow things to go too far. Usually this was no big deal, but what about special occasions? Anniversaries, birthdays, and weekly reunions didn't always fall into a "safe zone." We both started pushing the envelope on our "safe zones" until the recommended seven days of abstinence was whittled down to three. Just weeks after our first anniversary, I was "surprisingly" pregnant.

Erv's Bottom Line

* Being debt free is a glorious feeling.
* Job hunting is not fun, but God will bring opportunities amidst your persistence.
* A budget is you telling your money what you want it to do … not the other way around.
* A budget doesn't give you more money, but it will feel like it does.

- Work together to decide how you'll spend your money.

- Habits form from consistent behavior (if you want to change a bad habit or form a good habit, it will require you to practice).

- Money is not worth arguing over but priorities are. The good news, this is an infrequent conversation after setting your budget.

- Family is a gift. Treasure it well.

- A mission statement means putting your hopes, dreams, and goals in writing. This makes it more likely to happen.

- Keep dating- you should always keep the fire burning and the chase in process. Love like you did at the start.

- You can make plans – and humor God.

Chapter Six:

From Hell to Hope

The Dark Night of the Soul

Though we were both fully responsible for this unexpected blessing, this was not what either of us had planned. After a year of substituting for women on maternity leave, I was finally a prime candidate for my own classroom. In the meantime, Erv had decided to not finish his third year of seminary. While the church was willing to hire us for another year of youth ministry, I expected teaching full-time to be challenging enough, and Erv was no longer interested in pursuing ministry. The church hired someone else, and my teaching job didn't materialize (again). I left substitute teaching to work as a migrant teacher and decided to begin a master's degree. Erv got a low paying job at a home for special needs children. Our five-year savings plan came to a screeching halt.

All of these changes disheartened us both. I enjoyed my new teaching position, pushing into classrooms to help the children of migrant farmers. But now that I was pregnant, my dream of one day having my own classroom would be further delayed, since once the baby arrived, I didn't want to be working full time for at least a few years. Erv was going through his own disappointment. After investing two years into a seminary education, he no longer wanted to pursue ministry, and he didn't know what he wanted to do next. As a young college graduate with little experience, his job options were limited. He found working as a night-time aide at a residential facility for special needs children to be both demanding and depressing.

After a year of relative carefree marital bliss, our lives became stressed and our relationship strained. Our collective and individual dreams were falling apart. I worked all day traveling between three school districts while attending graduate school three nights a week. Erv worked the overnight shift which meant we rarely saw each other. We kept to our meager budget, but paying cash for grad school meant our rate of savings was minimal.

My ultimate dream had always been having children. I wanted so much to be excited about this new baby. One of my best friends had a 1year-old, and I enjoyed spending time with her and her son. The special bond they shared was one I'd always looked forward to- and I knew that Erv would be the kind of father I had always wanted growing up. I thought we would make a great parenting team. Unfortunately, the timing of the pregnancy seemed to be ruining everything.

One evening when I was finished with my night class, Erv and I went out for a walk. It was cool and dark and the first chill of fall hung in the air. These night time walks admiring the stars had always been a relaxing time for us to enjoy. This particular night, we felt more like enemies than friends. We blamed each other for this "mistake" and the consequences we were now facing. Our whole time frame was ruined, and our future had become completely uncertain. We both made rash statements we didn't mean. By the time we got home, I was in tears. Desperate for peace to return to our lives, I secretly prayed this pregnancy would end in a miscarriage. Maybe then our lives could return to normal.

I woke up early the next morning to extreme abdominal pain. Hours passed, and it would not subside. I asked Erv to take me to the hospital. He called our pastor and his wife, who met us at the emergency room. They prayed for us as doctors and nurses flitted in and out of my sterile, curtained area. They gave me a barrage of tests as my mind prepared for the worse. I pleaded with God to ignore my desperate prayer from the night before. We patiently waited for the test results. Finally, a grim-faced doctor entered the room and pulled his chair up alongside my bed.

"Your ultrasound shows no signs of life. I'm sorry. You should go home and get some rest."

Our heads swam as we took in the reality of this news. My mind searched for an alternate meaning to his words. Was there no hope at all? Could he possibly be wrong? Were there more tests they should perform? As I asked my questions, the doctor confirmed my fears. Our baby was gone. In a matter of moments, I'd gone from an expectant mother to an empty shell. As I slipped into the bathroom to change into my clothes, I wept bitter tears of regret.

Erv and I returned to our apartment in silence. Word of our miscarriage traveled quickly, and friends stopped by with flowers. I didn't want to see anyone. The phone rang, but we ignored it. I didn't want to talk to anyone. We sat alone in the dark. Within hours, the abdominal cramping grew worse. I sat in the middle of the living room floor with Erv's arms wrapped around me. The physical and emotional pain engulfed me like a dark cloud. We prayed and held each other, feeling the loss of a gift we'd shown little thankfulness for.

As we struggled through the night, we clung to each other. By morning, we were exhausted and resigned to the truth. We could not bring our baby back. We spent the day alone in our apartment again, repenting of our ungrateful hearts. All throughout the week, friends continued to bring us meals, flowers, and encouraging notes. As we read their words, we received their comfort and accepted God's forgiveness. At the end of the week, Erv and I took a hike to one of our favorite spots, Nichols tower. As the sun shone on our faces, we reflected on Psalm 30:5, "Weeping may stay for the night, but rejoicing comes in the morning." We decided that morning had come. Though our sadness remained, we would rejoice in our blessings and the future God had for us. We trusted He would give us children in His time.

Small Ventures and Big Changes

That time came sooner than we thought. After the extreme sadness of losing a baby, we were less than committed to preventing pregnancy. We weren't intentionally trying to get pregnant, but apparently, we didn't have to be. Within months of losing our first baby, we were pregnant with our second.

Life had just started returning to normal. We were both still working low paying jobs, paying for grad school, and trying to save all we could. Motivated to increase our earnings, Erv took another part-time job, and we invested in a multi-level marketing company. We attended rallies, sold products, and encouraged friends and family members to join our new business. With Erv's head for numbers and my sales savvy, we were off to a strong start. Within months, we were setting records within the company. We were the bright shining stars of our network. Surely we would advance quickly and fast track our way to our life goals.

Unfortunately, as we returned to our mission statement, we found ourselves convicted. We were spending every free moment promoting our business. Every conversation was focused on achieving success. Every relationship became a potential "contact." Our mission had become building a business, not building a kingdom. Erv also noticed that the money we were investing in products and promotional material was continuing to consume the majority of our profit. This business was costing us financially as well as spiritually. By spring, we became inactive in our new company. This was a big decision, but after talking and praying together, we agreed this was the right move for us. Erv's next decision, however, took me completely by surprise.

A failed businessman, an underpaid worker, and an expectant father, Erv was desperate for a change. We gave our landlords 30 days notice that we would be moving out. We were moving to Albany where we could be closer to Erv's family, and he could pursue an MBA. I was disappointed and angry. Oneonta was our home.

Our friends and church family were here. My migrant teaching job was here. My graduate school was here. I couldn't possibly pick up in the middle of all that and move.

Four weeks later, I was packing a moving truck. We had no jobs waiting for us. No apartment to live in. No church to attend. We simply picked up and left. We moved our things into Erv's mother's abandoned beauty shop. Erv got a job working with a temp agency in Albany. I continued to commute two hours to Oneonta each week, staying with a generous family from church. We stayed in Albany with Erv's mother on the weekends. As I finished out the school year, my pregnant belly started to show. Reminded of our recent loss, I chose to thank God for this baby. I felt defeated and lost, but I refused to let our circumstances steal my joy.

By the end of the school year, we managed to find a small basement apartment in downtown Troy. Our bedroom had no door and our soon-to-be baby's room was no bigger than a walk-in closet. The living room was so tiny we had to borrow a love seat from Erv's stepfather because our full-sized couch simply would not fit. He also gave us our first television- a used model with a 12 inch screen. Each night around 11 p.m., we would hear jingly songs from an ice cream truck out our back window. We were sure they were selling something other than ice cream at that hour of the night. The police frequented our neighborhood, and a drug house was shut down just a block from our apartment. This was not the dream environment I wanted for our new baby- but it was what we could afford.

Now that my migrant teaching job had come to an end, we brainstormed ways to continue paying our bills as well as saving for the future. Our budget remained stripped down to bare bones with no car payments, no cable bill, and no student loans. With Erv going back to graduate school, we would need another source of income. With my love for children and Erv's heart for entrepreneurship, we decided I should start my own home day care. I filed the necessary paperwork with the county and put up posters at the local grocery store. Within weeks I had my first customer- a single mother of two who worked full-time at the hospital across the street.

Since our apartment was so small, two children were all I could appropriately care for. The boys would get dropped off early in the morning. Erv would head out to work in our only car. I'd put the 9-month-old in his stroller while taking the 4-year-old by the hand. We'd walk the four blocks up to the local park, singing along the way. The last block was all up-hill- my four year old friend would help me push his brother as I strained to get the stroller and my pregnant belly up to the top. We'd spend a few hours at the park, and then head back to the apartment. After lunch, I'd put the boys napping in the living room while I rested on my bed. When we woke up, we had snack time, craft time, and play time. Their mom would pick them up just before dinner, and I would be completely exhausted.

Erv would come home from his temp job tired and frustrated. He'd spend most days writing names on files, alphabetizing folders, and performing other tasks requiring less than a high school education. He found the work so demeaning and mindless he wanted to "stick pencils in his eyes." Surely a college degree should be able to get him a better job than this! We'd watch an hour or two of local television after dinner, and then Erv would get some sleep before heading to his night job loading trucks at UPS. Working from 11 p.m. to 3 a.m. disrupted his sleep pattern, but this was the only part-time job he could find that provided benefits and fit around his 9 a.m. - 5 p.m. schedule.

I tried to remain supportive and encouraging, but Erv was in a downward spiral that seemed to have no end. Between the lack of sleep and frustrating job circumstances, he would unexpectedly burst into fits of anger. One day he punched a hole in our living room wall. Another day he dented our kitchen wall. I was especially scared when he became so angry he punched the windshield of our car. The impact of his wedding ring caused the whole window to crack. I sat pregnant in the passenger seat, staring at the cracked windshield in front of me. I wanted to run. I wanted to get out of the car, pack all my stuff, and move home with my mom. The only thing that stopped me was the knowledge that I would eventually forgive Erv, and my mom would not.

When I got home, I called a friend from Oneonta. A dear family from church had adopted us as their children. I spoke to our "dad" and told him what had happened. He talked with Erv and helped him get some perspective. He prayed with Erv, helping him to take a long-term view of our life and all God had already done. I was so thankful not to be alone in this situation.

Erv came to bed apologizing for what had happened. He asked me for forgiveness, and I granted it, as I knew I would. I had spent the last hour praying. God had taken away my fear and filled my heart with hope. I knew that He did not give us this baby to cause us further suffering. I was convinced that this expected child was a sign of better days to come. I would not allow our present struggles to cloud my hope in God's love for us.

I shared this with Erv as we lay in bed talking for what seemed like hours, appreciating the long talks after a difficult rift between us. We had committed long ago to, "not let the sun go down while we are still angry," as taught in Ephesians 4:26. With the baby's birth looming near, our conversation turned to a recurring theme- baby names. We had made some progress selecting names. This was an important decision to us. We believe that the naming of a child is an opportunity to wish character upon them. If it was a boy, we would name him Brandon, meaning "brave prince." His middle name would be Christopher, after our campus minister, whom we both loved and admired. If it was a girl her name would be Mikayla, meaning "one who is like God." Our struggle was choosing a girl's middle name. I longed to name her after my beloved grandmother Marjorie, but I could not bear the possibility of my daughter being called, "Large Marge."

After reflecting on the encouragement God had provided me earlier that night, I suggested to Erv that we use the middle name Hope if we had a girl. Then she would always remind us to keep our hope in God strong despite our circumstances. Erv loved this idea. I was touched when he told me that naming her Hope would be like naming her after me since I am always full of hope. We wanted our child to have a strong faith in God to sustain him or her through any challenges he or she might one day face. The name Hope would be a constant mark of that faith. After a trying evening and a long discussion, we slept peacefully in each other's arms, thankful to have renewed hope.

Special Delivery

The next several weeks turned to more joyful times. Erv started his MBA and had a vision for a real career. We experienced the generosity of friends and family once again as they blessed us with baby showers. We received a car seat, stroller, high chair, and baby swing. Erv's mom found us a great crib at a garage sale. My college roommate sewed beautiful Noah's Ark themed bedding and matching decorations for the walls. Family members and friends gave us a used playpen, baby clothes, bottles, and baby gates. As much as people told us that babies were expensive, we found that preparing for our first child came at little financial cost if we were willing to accept less than perfect hand-me-downs. We were quite sure the baby would not mind.

One of the best cost saving strategies we found preparing for this new baby was the use of cloth diapers. Disposable diapers are a huge ongoing cost. With cloth diapers, we purchase them once and then can reuse them over and over again. The cost of laundering them is much cheaper than buying disposable (if you wash them yourself and don't use a laundry service), and they are better for the environment. While we knew it would be inconvenient (and sometimes downright gross) to wash cloth diapers, we believed the savings and environmental benefits would be worth it.

We would soon put this theory to the test as my first contractions arrived right on my due date. They came slowly at first, then faster and faster. I alerted my mom, and she quickly came to town. Once she arrived, the contractions slowed down. I consulted my midwife, and she concluded that it was either very early labor or false labor. To keep ourselves distracted, we decided to enjoy one of our favorite fall activities, picking apples. We headed up to the local orchard with my mom, timing the contractions as we drove. She was shocked to see me climbing apple trees while nine months pregnant, in the early stages of labor. Erv and I were hopeful that the activity would move things along!

By early evening, things were indeed moving along. I sent Erv to bed to get some rest before what I expected to be a very long night. My mom and I watched television and played cards to help pass time. When the contractions got stronger, I stopped playing and mom would hold my hand while I used my breathing exercises to manage the pain. At 1 a.m., when the pain became severe and the contractions were only five minutes apart, I woke Erv.

We hopped in the car and headed to the hospital, or so I thought. I was lying in the back seat, in terrible pain. After only two minutes, the car came to a stop. I was annoyed when I looked up and saw we were at a gas station. All day long I had asked Erv to stop and buy gas. We knew I was in labor and would need to go to the hospital sometime that day. The car was on E and the hospital was a 20 minute drive away. Now we were in downtown Troy at 1 a.m. where the only people around were the gas station attendant, a prostitute, and her next potential customer. I wanted to get out of there, quickly.

We got back on the road and traveled for about 15 minutes. I had resumed my horizontal position in the back seat, yet my partially obscured view revealed that we still were not headed to the hospital. I sat up awkwardly and asked, "Where are you going?!" Erv blushed and confessed that he had gone into "auto-pilot" mode and driven to his night job at UPS. I replied, "They do deliver, but not babies. Get me to the hospital!"

We made a u-turn in the middle of the highway, my poor mom following behind us, not having a clue what was happening. She'd already followed us to the gas station and half-way to UPS. I was glad she hadn't given up and gone home! We finally arrived at the hospital and waited several more hours before the baby was ready to be born. I have never been so thankful to have Erv as my partner. He was by my side through every contraction, walking up and down the hospital corridors. Because we were committed to a natural delivery, my midwife had me constantly changing positions to keep me comfortable and keep the process moving forward. Erv held my hand, read me Scripture and prayed for me through the night and into the next day. At 5:38 p.m., Mikayla Hope Starr was finally born.

She has been filling us with hope ever since.

Erv's Bottom Line

- It is normal to face hard times.
- You will find yourself fighting with the one's you love most. Try to fight fair.
- It's all in the timing – just not our timing.
- Shared loss or suffering is a cement than can bond or break a relationship.
- Home is where your loved ones are.
- Don't be afraid of change.
- Joy is a choice (though it can be a hard one to make).
- When life is overwhelming we need the love and experience of others.
- When in despair, hope is a powerful comfort.
- Names matter.
- Expensive baby supplies are not for the baby.
- Never leave the car on empty – especially with a pregnant wife at home.

Chapter Seven:

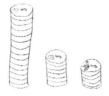

Get Rich Slow Schemes

A Mother's Love

As soon as Mikayla was born, they laid her in my arms. She pooped all over me. Not just ordinary poop. A baby's first poop-black and tar-like. It's basically the most disgusting kind of poop on earth. I had just survived 21 hours of labor, and I was covered with "first poop." This was my welcome to motherhood. I didn't even care. Mikayla was the most beautiful thing I had ever seen.

I was honestly a little surprised. Not that I assumed Erv and I would make ugly babies -- I had simply been conditioned to expect a less-than-perfect baby. When you go through child labor classes, they show you picture after picture of scary looking babies. You are instructed not to expect a beautiful baby. Being a good listener, I was prepared to meet a cone-head, prune-faced, hairy baby. Instead, my baby had a perfectly round head, the slightest bit of light brown hair, big blue eyes, and a perfect little smile. Yes, Mikayla was born smiling. Some say it was gas, but I know better.

As the nurses struggled to scrape the poop off my stomach, I looked down at her perfect little face. "It's you. You're finally here." The moment I spoke, she turned her little head and looked right at me. It's a moment I will never forget. She knew me. She recognized my voice. She was as happy to meet me as I was to meet her!

I held her through the night. I held her through the next day. By the second night, the nurses insisted I send her to the nursery for a little while so I could get some rest. I lay alone in my hospital bed thinking about her. Those perfect little fingers. Those big blue eyes. That precious smile. An hour later, I asked them to bring her back to me. I missed her.

I always knew my mother loved me. She had told me almost every day my whole life. She had this little joke. She'd say, "Remember, I don't like you. I love you." She would write this to me in birthday cards and whisper it in my ear before I went to sleep at night. She showed me her love in action. She drove me to school because I hated taking the bus. She made me lunch because I hated buying it at school. She sat on the side of my bed when I was sick. She would read me stories and put a bendy straw in my Coke so I could sip it lying down.

I was spoiled. Not with possessions. Those were quite limited. I was spoiled with love. It was an unconditional love that seemed to have no end. Now that I was a mother, I realized just how loved I was. I was crazy in love with Mikayla. I would do anything for her. And I had known her for only two days. How much more did my mom love me? She had loved me for 24 years. The thought overwhelmed me.

My mom stayed with us for the first two weeks after Mikayla came home from the hospital. She was very helpful, and I was extremely grateful. The adjustment to parenthood was a bit awkward for us. It was actually easier for Erv. Being the oldest of four siblings, he had cared for younger children most of his life. His brother Adam is 16 years younger. Erv had changed diapers, given baths, and was very comfortable around babies. I loved children but had never taken care of a newborn. Mikayla seemed so tiny and fragile to me.

I remember calling the pediatrician to make Mikayla's first doctor's appointment. "Yes, I need to make an appointment for my (choke, pause) daughter." The word felt so foreign coming out of my mouth. *I* was the daughter, not the mother. Erv and I both felt like we were babysitting someone else's child. At 24, neither of us felt old enough to be legitimate parents. We kept expecting Mikayla's real parents to show up any minute, ready to take her home. After about two weeks, the reality set in. No one was coming to pick her up. This kid was ours to stay.

And Baby Makes Three

During our pre-marital counseling, we had been told that a having a baby did not make you a family. We learned that, as soon as you got married, you were a family- children would be welcome additions to your existing family. We wanted to love our baby and give her everything she needed, but we did not want to neglect our relationship with each other. We had seen this misstep in other marriages, and we were determined to avoid it. Instead, we included Mikayla in our present lifestyle, a welcome addition to the Starr family.

We brought Mikayla on walks, hikes, and bike rides. We took her to the movies, plays, and parties. Once, we put her to sleep in a bedroom at Erv's brother's Super Bowl party with a rowdy crowd cheering in the living room next door. She was so accustomed to this practice of falling asleep in a strange, noisy place she slept right through the whole party. Our pastor's wife used to joke that Mikayla would one day write a book entitled, "My Life in a Car Seat," because we dragged our poor kid so many places due to our active lifestyle.

We did make sure to reserve some time for just the two of us. Living near family was especially helpful. Grandparents, aunts, and uncles were so anxious to spend time with Mikayla, they practically shoved us out the door to go on dates. This was a blessing. But even when family was not available, I found that child care exchange with other young moms was easy and helpful. I would watch a friend's child one day, and she would watch mine the next. We didn't pay for babysitting the first six years of Mikayla's life!

Even with free babysitting, we still tried to keep the weekly dates cheap. We frequently enjoyed walks in Frear Park, the dollar movie theatre (a fantastic Albany find!), and Cracker Barrel. It was during this stage of our marriage that Cracker Barrel became my favorite restaurant. Here was our Cracker Barrel strategy- We would put our name on the list to be seated and browse in the gift shop while we waited. We wouldn't buy anything, but I'd get cool ideas of craft stuff I could make for Christmas and birthday presents. Once seated, we would order dessert or hot drinks. If you like the atmosphere of eating out (which we did since we lived in a tiny basement apartment), getting dessert or coffee instead of dinner still gets you out to a nice place but cuts your bill significantly. For us, it was less about the food and more about the experience. After dessert we would sit in front of the fireplace on the stone hearth and play checkers. This is an acceptable practice at Cracker Barrel. They leave the checker boards out, inviting you to enjoy them. We would casually chat by the crackling fire, acting as if this was our very own living room. It was a wonderful place to escape and enjoy- a favorite date for about $5.

The Cost of Convenience

I didn't pay to feed Mikayla for months. Please don't call Child Protective Services. I was committed to nurse my baby and successfully did so for six months. I realize that it is not for everyone. It is however, excellent food for the baby, helps you get back into shape, and is totally and completely free. Formula, on the other hand, is expensive! That's why they give it to you for free at the hospital. During the first three weeks of nursing, I was tempted to give it up many times- usually in the middle of the night when Erv was peacefully sleeping. That free can of formula would call to me from the cupboard, "C-a-r-r-i-e! I'm here w-a-i-t-i-n-g. You know you want to come o-p-e-n me and let Erv feed the b-a-b-y!"

I was determined NOT to open that can of formula. I refused to start a habit that would cost our family an extra $10 to $15 a week simply for convenience. Not when I could feed Mikayla for free (and get my flat tummy back without a gym membership).

The same temptation came with disposable diapers. They send these home from the hospital with you for free too. These companies aren't stupid. They know if they can get you to start a habit of using their product, you'll keep buying it until your child is potty trained in two to three years. There were many days when I was on my knees, swishing a poopy cloth diaper out in the toilet, that I would imagine myself simply tossing a neat, tidy disposable diaper into the trash can. These were the moments when I would train my mind to move from this image to a picture of myself at the grocery store checkout, paying $20 a week for diapers that would end up sitting in a landfill until Mikayla went off to college 18 years later. I stuck to the cloth diapers.

The cloth diaper commitment required additional resolve since we did not own a dryer. Erv's mother and step-father had given us a washing machine for Christmas, but we couldn't afford a dryer. In many ways this was a blessing. We did a fair amount of laundry, and the cost of running the dryer would have added up quickly as well. We had three collapsible dryer racks instead. These would be lined up side by side in our living room, each one full of white, cloth rectangles. Given the size of our tiny living room, the space was literally wall to wall diapers twice a week.

When Mikayla started eating solid food, we once again found old-fashioned ideas to be most economical. Instead of buying jars of baby food, I would cook simple ingredients like carrots, apples, broccoli, etc. Once the item was cooked, I would put it in the blender with a little water until it had the consistency of baby food. Next, I would spoon the mushy food into ice cube trays, cover them with plastic wrap, and place the trays in the freezer. When it was time to eat, I would pop out a single cube of the food I wanted and heat it up. As Mikayla's appetite grew, I took out more cubes. By the time Mikayla was old enough to start eating table food, I purchased a simple food processor (that you crank by hand) at a garage sale for $5. When we ate our meals, I would put some of whatever food we were eating into the processor. Erv and I would take turns mixing Mikayla's food. This also helped Mikayla become accustomed to the taste of the food our family typically eats. We were committed early on to help our children not be picky eaters. Since most child-friendly convenience foods are pre-packaged, unhealthy, and expensive, we wanted to avoid them.

In general, we found that going ahead and "sweating the small stuff" saved us money every time. When we went out for the day as a family, we would pack our own food, avoiding the high priced food at concession stands and fast food joints. We frequently carried water bottles to avoid buying drinks on the run. Erv packed peanut butter and jelly sandwiches for work every day. When he came home, I would rinse out the plastic baggie and use it again. We found that buying the store brand was almost always as good as the name brand. If we preferred a name brand, we'd use a coupon or wait for it to go on sale and stock up. We bought things in bulk and divided them up into reused canning jars to keep them fresh. I lined up these jars on my counter, finding the variety of textures and colors to make an attractive display.

My decorating style in general was a mix of garage sale finds and common use items creatively displayed. Maybe it was all of that time hanging out at Cracker Barrel, but I'd display kitchen utensils, old flags, and pictures from outdated calendars on my walls. We'd also bring the outdoors in. Dried wildflowers would lie along windowsills and plant cuttings from a friend's house thrived in ceramic bowls made in high school shop class. The best part of the low-cost decorating was providing a stress-free environment for raising a baby. I never worried about Mikayla breaking my china vase or soiling our expensive furniture.

We found this stage of being poor to be the best time to have a baby. When it came to clothes and toys, if she didn't have the very best, she didn't know what she was missing. Her very first Christmas, we didn't buy her a single present. It wasn't because we didn't love her, but because it seemed a waste of money. At two months old, she certainly didn't feel she was being robbed of the perfect Christmas. If we saved that money, it would be worth more when she was older and actually cared. Just having a baby with us for the first time at Christmas was a priceless gift.

Increasing our Earnings

A penny saved is, indeed, a penny earned. We were experiencing that truth daily and enjoyed watching those pennies add up in our bank account. We continued to look for ways to add to it. Loading trucks at night no longer worked with Erv in grad school and a new baby in the house. Always on the lookout for new opportunities, Erv found a company that promised big commissions for little effort. He went through the interview process, a rigorous training program, and finally purchased his demonstration products. Similar to our first business venture, Erv was booking appointments with friends and family, this time trying to sell them high priced knives. He worked hard at it, looking for the promised big payout equaling his effort. After months of working a traditional job, taking night classes, and making sales calls, we came to the conclusion that there is no such thing as, "get rich quick." Disciplined effort to make sacrificial choices over and over again is what would eventually move us from our current situation to a place of financial stability. We reminded ourselves that each dollar we saved today would be invested and multiplied in our future.

It was at this time of financial struggle that we started a retirement account. Investing in your retirement at your mid-20s allows that account to double many more times as opposed to waiting until you are financially comfortable in your 30s or 40s. We did not wait until we had "extra" money to invest. We made sacrifices and started investing in our future as soon as possible. We didn't want the pressing needs of today to overshadow our long term plans.

Education was our other strategic investment. Committed to avoid debt, pursuing a masters degree was a calculated risk. We knew that attaining advanced degrees would open doors of opportunity for us. Up to this point, we had paid for all of our graduate courses with cash. By the end of Erv's first semester working on his MBA, he got an idea. While looking at the course catalog, he realized that the only difference in coursework for an MBA and PhD was a little thing called a "dissertation." "How hard could that be?" Erv surmised. He immediately applied for a doctorate program in Organizational Management.

Excited about this new course of action, Erv anxiously awaited the results of his application. He studied up on the program, discovering he would learn about managing not only for-profit businesses but also public and non-profit organizations. This was a perfect fit as yet another door of opportunity opened to Erv. In less than one year, his temp job writing names on file folders had evolved into the accounts receivable manager position for a small, local company. Erv was pleased with the promotion but was dissatisfied with receiving temp worker pay for a job with significant responsibility. He requested a raise but was told the company could not afford to pay him more. Always on the lookout for other options, Erv had taken civil-service exam months earlier. He performed well on the test and was offered a position in county government. When he tendered his resignation at his current job, they offered him a raise. Erv was not impressed by their lack of integrity, suddenly having the money to give him a raise. (This company incidentally went out of business a few years ago due to fraud.)

As Erv got accustomed to his new job at the county, I was struggling with mine. Many women find caring for small children while raising their own to be rewarding and convenient. This was not my experience. With three small children in my care, our tiny apartment was extremely crowded. Between the dryer racks, playpens, and high chairs, we could barely move from room to room. Nap time was nothing short of a disaster. As soon as I would get one baby to sleep, the other would cry, and wake the first one up. I'd get both babies to sleep, and the 4 year old would start singing or throw a toy into his brother's crib. And there was no escaping the house.

The winter snow piled high on the un-shoveled city sidewalks, making them impassible with the stroller. Driving was not an option since Erv was gone at work with the only car. I tried bundling up all three children for a walk to the park. I carried one baby in the backpack, the other in the front pack, and the four year old walked along by my side. Carrying two babies in full snow suits while tromping through a foot of snow across four city blocks is not easy. By the time I got to the top of the final hill, I was covered with sweat. We reached the park and the 4-year-old took off running. I chased after him, babies bouncing in front and behind me. Mikayla started crying, and I collapsed on a park bench. I yelled for my 4-year-old friend to come to me, "NOW!" Thankfully, he obeyed.

Mikayla was hungry. While I was committed to nursing, this was not a convenient time or place to get this done. I was sitting on the bench with a fidgety preschooler on one side of me and a propped-up toddler on the other. Trying to feed Mikayla discreetly through three layers of winter clothing while managing to stay warm and modest was a feat. Fortunately, both boys stayed still until Mikayla was finished and I could get up from the bench and push all three of them on the child swings. The winter wind seemed to cut right through my clothing. Not wanting to be responsible for another woman's children getting frostbite, I packed the kids up, and we walked back through the snow to the apartment. That was the last day I ventured outside with the children all winter. It simply wasn't worth it.

By spring, I had closed my child care business. Erv and I had started volunteering with the youth ministry at our new church, and I loved it. Working with those teenagers was the highlight of my week. Ever since Erv quit seminary, I had told him he would never be satisfied outside of ministry. I realized it was not Erv who would miss being in ministry, it was me. I longed to do something of eternal value that also allowed me to be a full-time parent. I applied for a job with Campus Ambassadors, the same organization that had been so instrumental to building our faith while in college.

I was thrilled to be appointed as a campus minister in May! I would be starting a new ministry at the University at Albany. This was scary and intimidating, but I was up for the challenge. In the meantime, Erv got less exciting news from the same university. They denied his application for the PhD program. He had excellent grades, GMAT scores, and references. The problem was his essay. Always frank about his feelings, Erv had shared that his career goals were to become a small business owner and a college professor. They wanted to see greater passion for research. He had none. Erv was discouraged at this rejection.

I remember bringing him the letter during his lunch break at work. Erv had given me the car for the day so I could grocery shop. I stopped by his office on the way home from the store. We sat in the parking lot on the hood of the car, enjoying the warm spring day. It was such a pleasant moment, I hated to ruin it with the letter, but I had no choice. I am terrible at pretending, and Erv knew something was up. I gave him the letter so he could read it for himself. He was angry and disappointed. Fortunately, we were in a public place so he maintained pretty good self-control. We talked for a while, and then Erv headed back in to work. I drove home crying tears of disappointment for him.

One of Erv's greatest strengths is that he does not take "no" for an answer. Refusing to give up, he stayed in the MBA program, carefully selecting courses that would fulfill the MBA or the PhD. He would reapply to the PhD program in the fall after making strategic connections in the department. He would also rewrite his essay to show greater interest in research.

After a few months working in the Department for Youth at the county, a position opened up in the Department of Economic Development. This position was intriguing to Erv. It would allow him to see the whole process of starting a new business from a different vantage point. He would also learn about government planning and the establishment of roads, buildings, and neighborhoods. He admired the director of this department as a person of character and integrity, knowing he could learn a lot from him. Erv was chosen for the position, and we celebrated the new job- and the raise that came along with it.

We approached our second year in Albany excited about these opportunities. We both had new careers, our baby was healthy and growing, and our savings was finally starting to accumulate. We felt a sense of progress and achievement. As we celebrated Mikayla's first birthday, I realized I needed to talk to Erv about something important, preferably in public.

Erv's Bottom Line

* We've said to each other many times, "I love you always and I like you most of the time."

* One of the best gifts you can give your children is the safety of them knowing you love your spouse. They are a welcome addition to your family.

✖ Let your child be blessed by having other adults in their lives from the start.

✖ You can eat at home and get dessert out – not just the other way around.

✖ Living within your means may mean being different or letting go of conveniences (e.g. disposable diapers or new baby items)

✖ Sweating the small stuff adds up.

✖ Having a baby doesn't have to cost a lot.

✖ Struggle can teach good habits.

✖ Building wealth (for most of us) will be a slow process of consistent saving, or not happen at all.

✖ Some of your money today should be invested to work for you tomorrow. Some of what you earn is for bread (today), seed (tomorrow), and to be harvested (to bless others).

✖ Master's degrees and Ph.D. programs are not the same. A Dissertation is a long arduous research project – well suited for academics, but not so for practitioners.

✖ Childcare can give you a great workout ☺

✖ This world is not eternity. Don't let yourself get trapped into always thinking it is. This is not to say it is un-important. It is important, but it's not everything.

✖ Rejection and failure are part of the journey. And remember, life can change dramatically in 12 months – don't give up when it seems hopeless (the dawn is coming).

✖ When giving men bad/unexpected/unwanted/ disappointing…news – do it in public.

Chapter Eight:

House Hunters

Good News and Landmines

The longer you are married, the more you learn about your spouse. This seems pretty obvious. The challenge is to adapt and adjust in response to what you learn. It's easy to simply do things the way you've always done them, or want to do them, regardless of what works for your spouse. This is a very bad idea. Your ever growing storehouse of knowledge about your partner can be used to bless your spouse and maybe even make your life more pleasant at the same time. The choice is yours to make ... do what comes naturally or be wise and adjust accordingly.

When I have news, my instinct is to blurt it out as soon as possible. If you have news you want shared with as many people as possible, just tell me. I am happy to tell the world on your behalf. If you have a secret that you don't want leaked until a very special time, to a very special person, please don't tell me without first saying: This is a secret... I'm happy to find out when it becomes public knowledge along with everyone else. I'm not saying that I am in the habit of betraying a confidence. I am capable of keeping others' secrets and have several that I refuse to tell. It's just my natural inclination to share news. I am a sharer. That's who I am.

This is especially true when it comes to my own news. When it's my birthday, I tell everyone. The mailman. The teller at the bank. The grocery store clerk. Basically, anyone willing to listen to me. When I got my new job with Campus Ambassadors, I spent days on the phone sharing my joy. When I got my braces off, I sent pictures of my new-found teeth to everyone I know. I enjoy writing those newsy Christmas letters that tell all your friends and family everything you've done over the past year. I am an effervescent, good news sharer.

On a beautiful fall day in 1996, I had news to share. Good news that should be celebrated with the world. But I knew better. I had been married to Erv for three years now. We had been friends for twice that long. There is a time and place to share news with Erv. I cannot blurt out things when they first come to me. I need to wait until he can hear about it, and I must think about how he will react. His reaction is somewhat within my control by my choosing where and how I tell him things... If I share news with Erv the moment he gets home from work after a long, hard day, he will not receive it well. If I blurt out my excitement when he clearly has news of his own to share, then I will steal his thunder. If he is tired, he will be sound asleep before I get to the climax of my story. I have learned to patiently wait to share my news until the perfect time when Erv can be as excited as I am.

I have also learned that good news to me is not always good news to Erv. Giving Erv news that he might think is bad can be complicated. When I think of times when I have shared bad news with Erv the phrase, "don't shoot the messenger," comes to mind. Anger can be an unpleasant reaction to bad news, and I had been the subject of Erv's misplaced anger more than once. I avoid it whenever I can. Outbursts of anger were like landmines that I had learned to distinguish and carefully navigate around. Sometimes, however, I had no choice but to head straight for them.

A landmine was inevitably in my path. I had news that would make Erv upset. Our plans that were finally falling into place were about to get turned upside down again. He had just recently recovered from the rejection to the Ph.D. program. Was he ready to deal with another blow? As I thought about delivering that rejection letter last spring, I realized an important lesson was learned that day. I had brought it to him at lunch because I didn't want to wait until he came home. It wasn't an intelligent decision but an impulsive one. His reaction taught me to be more strategic with my "news telling." Erv had demonstrated self-control in the face of that rejection because we were in public. He didn't lose his temper with other people around. By the time he had come home and we were in private, he had had plenty of time to calm down and be rational about it. Since I knew I was likely to get a strong reaction to this latest piece of news, I decided to share it with him on the Campus Ambassadors fall retreat. We would be in a setting focused on our Christian faith, and there would be lots of people around.

I patiently kept the news to myself until the second day of the retreat. We were standing just outside of the large meeting hall when I bravely stepped on the mine. "Do you remember when you were in high school, and you would pick teams in gym class? Sometimes you were the captain and got to pick who was on your team. Other times, people got put on your team, and they were not your choice. You had to try your best to win the game with the team you were given." This was my attempt at a "word picture," a technique taught to us by our small group leaders at church. It was supposed to help you communicate your feelings with your spouse. Sports analogies in general seemed to work well with Erv. "Well, God has given us another member to be on our team. And we need to be thankful for him or her and make it work."

"Are you pregnant again?!" was his immediate and startled response. He had gotten pretty good at interpreting my word pictures. I was impressed, but also nervous.

"Um, yep," was my elegant-with-words-under-pressure reply.

We are clearly very good at getting pregnant. This was the third time in three years. I waited for the angry outburst. There was only silence. I longed for a happy, joyful reaction, but I was content. We were trying to get back on our five year plan. We had been thrown off course multiple times, but we were finally making what felt like forward progress. That evening, I was shocked when he publicly shared our news with everyone on the Campus Ambassadors retreat! He asked for people to celebrate with us and keep us in their prayers. I thanked God for answering my prayers for a favorable reaction. Not only had Erv stayed calm, but he had acted in very "Carrie-like" fashion, sharing our news as soon as possible with everyone he could. I guess we both were learning a thing or two about each other.

Working Mom and Dr. Dad

When we returned home from the retreat, we received more good news. Erv was accepted into the PhD program! His excellent performance on his MBA coursework, his networking with decision makers at the University, and an updated essay which included research plans had changed people's minds, and now Erv was an official doctoral candidate. This would not be the last time we learned that persistence paid off. Erv continued taking classes at the University at Albany in the evening, while working at the county during the day. I had begun working at the University at Albany two days and two evenings a week doing campus ministry, usually taking Mikayla with me. To keep from passing like ships in the night, Erv would come home from work for lunch or meet me on campus where we'd enjoy packed sandwiches and quality family time every single day.

Little Mikayla was a big hit on campus. I'd bring her in the baby backpack and stand it up on a table in the student union. I'd sit at the table and chat with students on their way to and from classes. She loved watching all the commotion, and the students absolutely adored her. Female students especially would stop in their tracks to comment on her big blue eyes. "Oh, my gosh! She is so beautiful!" was a common response as students spotted her on their way to lunch. She was a fantastic conversation starter as I looked to establish a brand new Campus Ambassadors ministry on this state university campus of 20,000. I did have one skeptical student criticize me for bringing my baby to campus just so people would talk to me. My calm response, "Actually, I'm just cheap. I can't afford childcare, and I enjoy having her with me. How do you feel about working mothers?" This opened up a wonderful conversation with a total stranger about his close relationship with his working mom. He became a regular, stopping by my table to chat each week.

I never thought I'd like being a working mom. My dream was to stay home with my children as my own mom did. I was so thankful that God had provided a way to do both. As Mikayla got bigger, I would take her to campus in the stroller. I was given the kind that you could adjust to recline, and she would nap in the stroller while I would teach afternoon Bible studies. When she started walking and running, my students enjoyed taking her for tours around campus and showing her off at their dorm rooms. Because I was able to take Mikayla to work with me, I was there for her first words, her first steps, and her first ice cream cone. These were special moments I didn't want to miss. I know not all moms have the opportunity to do this, so I was especially thankful to be a full-time parent while pursuing a part-time career. While I didn't make a lot of money with this job, I was glad to be contributing something to our family income while raising our children and working a job I loved.

Erv was thankful for my contribution but still felt the stress of providing for our family while attending grad school and trying to save for a business. I could go back to teaching but that would mean paying for child care. The increased earnings would be cancelled out by the child care costs, purchasing dress clothes, and other related expenses. I would also miss out on being with our babies. Erv could work a second job, but he was already so busy with work and grad school. I wanted our children to grow up knowing their father, and he was committed to being involved in their lives. This meant we needed to find another way to earn money that didn't require either of us working more. I thought it was impossible. My visionary husband thought differently.

For Rent

Always the financially savvy one, Erv had a plan that would earn us money and save us money at the same time. It sounded too good to be true. What could this silver bullet be? Rental property. With our cheap living and constant saving, we had finally squirreled away enough for a meager down payment on an inexpensive house. Our tiny basement apartment didn't have sufficient space to accommodate a second child, and I was also anxious to get away from the mice, roaches, and other critters that shared our home underground. It was time to move! Our dream of owning a house was about to come true, but it would look much different than the "American Dream" house. We started looking at underpriced multi-family homes in need of repair.

The next several weeks involved searching real estate ads and driving all over God's creation with our real estate agent. The places we explored were either side-by-side duplexes, up –and-downstairs apartment houses, or multi-unit apartment houses. By purchasing one of these homes, we could live in our own unit and rent out the others, which would in turn help pay our mortgage. The more units the house had, the more income it could provide. Erv was in favor of a three-to-four family situation, maximizing our earning potential. Of course, more units also meant more work finding renters, more upkeep on the property, and more possible problems. We looked at many, many properties, considering carefully what we wanted as a family as well as a good rental location. Erv kept a close eye on the numbers. The sale price itself was less a factor than its relationship to the rental income. We were looking for an affordable price where the rental income would cover the mortgage.

We decided to purchase a three-family home located on the east side of Troy. It had been on the market for more than a year, so the price was significantly discounted. This new home got us out of the dangerous, high crime neighborhood in which we currently lived. It also gave us more room as a family. It was a large green colonial with white shutters and a front porch -- perfect for the wooden swing Erv made me for Christmas. There were two small apartments on the first floor and a large two bedroom apartment on the second floor. We excitedly moved in on the second floor. The house came with a double carport and a very small backyard for the kids. Mikayla's bedroom was larger than her previous "closet-sized" room, which was good since she would soon be sharing with her younger sibling.

We had been told our next baby was a girl, but were cautioned, "Don't paint." We took this to mean, they didn't really know. Two girls sharing a bedroom would be convenient.

I was excited that our new apartment had a dining room and a larger living room, and our bedroom actually had a door. Now that we had more space, we moved our stored furniture out of Erv's mom's house. She had been using our second-hand couch and found it more comfortable than her recently purchased living room set She decided to give us her new hunter green couch and chair, which was the first time we ever owned "new" furniture. I was thrilled! Our apartment also had hardwood floors and beautiful woodwork around all of the windows and doors. There was space for the washing machine right in the kitchen and Erv's mom blessed us with a used dryer that we kept out on the enclosed back porch. I was extremely thankful to have a new home for our growing family.

We inherited a renter in one first floor apartment from the previous owners, and Erv's cousin moved into the other. We didn't even need to place an advertisement to start earning income on the house. The rental earnings were enough to cover our mortgage, and we enjoyed living in our new home for free. After comparing interest rates, Erv decided to take the subsidized loans he was offered for his Ph.D. program. While we were opposed to incurring debt, we would take this money and pay extra on our mortgage each month. Since extra payments are applied directly toward the principle, the interest paid would be cut, as well as the length of the mortgage. The interest rate on our mortgage was higher than the interest rate on the school loans. It made sense to use one to pay off the other. We knew this wasn't our long-term home. When we sold it in the future, we could use the income from the sale to pay off the school loans, and we'd have saved thousands of dollars along the way.

We've found that most people don't consider living in a multi-family home a viable housing option. Most of us picture having our own little (or big) house, all to ourselves. For us, it has been one of our best money savers. It has also been a wonderful way to share our lives with others. We loved having Erv's cousin downstairs, and Suzy (our other renter) was a delight to get to know. She became a wonderful friend and an "adopted aunt" to Mikayla. We would occasionally have our renters over for dinner or invite them for special events like Christmas parties and BBQs. An added bonus to developing a relationship with our tenants was rent paid on time and infrequent complaints about minor issues like clogged toilets. Our friends didn't want to inconvenience our family and would address issues on their own whenever they could.

Do It Yourself

When you read a real estate listing, "good" condition means "not good" and our house was affordable because it was in "good" condition. Our home was considered a "handyman's special." There were several significant things that needed to be addressed. Our goal was to fix up the house while living in it so we could resell it for a profit. We've found that doing work ourselves is a considerable money saver. Our biggest challenge was the west inside wall running the length of the living room and dining room. The house was more than 100 years old and the wall had started to visibly lean out. Our engineers' inspection stated that this was not a structural concern. This was normal as the house had settled over the years. Erv's dad, who is also a general contractor, agreed with this conclusion. We were comfortable with the leaning wall, but we knew a potential buyer in the future would be concerned about it. With Erv's dad's help, we built another wall in front of it for support to give a little more peace of mind to would-be buyers. While we had little experience hanging sheetrock and mudding walls, we decided we couldn't make the wall look worse and were motivated by saving money. It came out pretty decent.

Over time, we moved on to painting both the interior and the exterior of the house. Paint is my favorite renovation tool. You get the biggest impact for the smallest investment. This is especially true if you aren't fussy about color. If you're flexible, you can get "mis-tinted" paint for a fraction of the cost of a custom color. This is paint that was tinted for a previous customer, but the customer decided not to buy it once it was mixed. There was always a can of "mis-tint" behind the counter that would work somewhere in the house. This paint is not usually on display so you'll need to ask what they have. When painting the exterior, we bought in bulk. Buying paint in a five gallon bucket is cheaper than buying it in one gallon cans. With large projects, this is the way to go. We also increased the value of our discount home by installing a clearance piece of linoleum in the kitchen and replacing the 30 year old roof. These projects were done with free labor from friends, family, and yours truly. I did not go up on the roof pregnant, but that's about it. I love a project and have trouble just watching while other people work.

The spring semester was wrapping up, and my pregnant status was coming to an end. Two weeks before my due date, the contractions started. Surprised, I called my mom, who arrived two hours later. We took 20-month-old Mikayla for long walks in the stroller, played marathon games of Monopoly, and watched late night movies. When things did not progress, I made myself try and get some sleep. By 5 a.m., I was too uncomfortable to rest. I got up and took a walk while everyone else slept. I had left a note and my mom came and found me an hour later. I guess she couldn't sleep either. I waited as long as possible before going to the hospital. Mom stayed home with Mikayla when Erv and I finally headed out. Our daughter Brianna took as long to arrive as her big sister had. It was 8:38 p.m. before she made her debut. Mom delayed putting Mikayla to bed so she could meet her new sister. They arrived at the hospital just as Brianna was born.

Mikayla was Brianna's very first visitor. She climbed up onto the bed with me, admiring her little sister. She was fascinated with Brianna's eyes. In fact, we had to keep her from poking them out of Brianna's little head. Just a toddler herself, Mikayla longed to touch all things bright and shiny. This special sister visit was brief as I hadn't even delivered the placenta yet. A nurse escorted Mikayla and my mother out to the crowded waiting room with the rest of our friends and family. I'm so glad we had Mikayla and my mom come in for that brief visit immediately after Brianna was born. Once they left the room, things went terribly wrong.

Erv's Bottom Line

* Marriage will require some change. But in general, who you marry is who you get. So be sure you can live with the person as they are, while hoping for the best.

* A friend defined anger as the result of a blocked dream or goal. Self-control might then be defined as not hurting others in one's anger. Self-control is a great gift to give your spouse. Train your children in it.

* Many times the answer "No" just means try again. Persistence is a good trait.

* Mixing work and parenting is a challenge. There is no "right" answer, but balancing the two can be overwhelming.

* Sharing your home can make home ownership much more affordable.

* It is better to earn interest, than to pay interest.

* Paint can make big changes for a small cost. Don't forget to ask about mis-tint paint.

* Treasure today. You don't know which day will be your last to enjoy someone or something.

Chapter Nine:

Trouble in Tents

Danger Zone

I remember being confused when Mikayla was born. After holding her for about five minutes, they took her away from me so I could deliver the placenta. I consider myself to be a pretty good listener, but I didn't remember hearing about this in childbirth classes. In all of the movies they showed, the woman went through labor, the baby was born, and that was the end. I did not recall anyone delivering a placenta. I was so exhausted after 20 hours of labor, I was not interested in delivering anything else. Ignoring my lack of enthusiasm, the nurses told me to push. After three good pushes, the placenta was out, and they had put Mikayla back in my arms. It turned out to be no big deal. This was not what happened with Brianna.

During Mikayla's visit with baby Brianna, my doctor patiently waited. She knew this was an important moment for our family, but she was concerned that I deliver the placenta. As soon as Mikayla and my mom left the room, I began pushing. Nothing happened. I pushed some more. Nothing. Another 30 minutes passed, and the placenta was not budging. I was frustrated and tired but oblivious to the danger I was in. Erv, however, had noticed the atmosphere in the room change. Our doctor's face had gone from calm and joyful to stressed and concerned. Erv also watched as a large basin that had been placed underneath me was filling up with blood. He wasn't training to become a medical doctor, but he knew this was not good. He kept his worried thoughts to himself and spoke only calm, encouraging words to me.

Once an hour passed after Brianna's birth, everything in the room changed. Suddenly, there was a flurry of activity as medical personnel rushed into the room, surrounding me. I was being given medication as my doctor explained that the placenta would need to be surgically removed. I had lost too much blood, and they couldn't wait any longer. Depending on the damage to my uterus, she may have to perform a hysterectomy. My brain struggled to process what was happening. I had just celebrated the birth of a healthy baby girl. Now I was being rushed to the operating room and may never give birth again. As they wheeled me away in my hospital bed, I searched for Erv. I could not see him anywhere. I lost consciousness and everything went black.

I woke up confused and disoriented. A nurse offered me a sip of orange juice from a straw. Where was I? Where were Erv and my baby? I spotted a clock on the wall. It was one in the morning. I had missed hours of precious bonding time with Brianna. I was sad and angry. The orange juice nurse disappeared, and I needed her. I wanted to see my husband ...and my baby ... and my mom ... and my husband's mom. I wanted to know if I still had a uterus. Would I ever give birth again? Why did this happen to me? Where was that blasted orange juice nurse? Was there a button somewhere I could push? Maybe I should just yell. I was too tired to yell. I closed my eyes and prayed.

I felt someone touch my left arm, and I looked up. It wasn't the orange juice nurse. It was Erv. I felt an incredible sense of relief. He had been in the nursery, feeding Brianna. He had been holding her and caring for her the past few hours. Our family and friends had met Brianna in the nursery, and now they had all gone home. Our baby was healthy and doing well. And I still had a uterus. They were able to remove the placenta without even doing surgery. I was relieved and thankful. And I wanted to see my baby.

Erv stayed with me in the recovery room for about 30 minutes. They moved me to a private room and sent Erv home to get some rest. I drifted in and out sleep, longing to see Brianna. I could barely remember what she looked like. My time with her had been so short. Would I recognize her when I finally got to hold her? Would she be willing to nurse after having a bottle? I wished I were able to get up and go see her. At 4 a.m., they finally brought little Brianna to my room. It was dark, and I could hardly see her. She was so tiny and cute. She nursed just fine and then slept peacefully in my arms. When the nurse came in an hour later, I did not want to let her go.

In the morning, they brought me to a shared room in the maternity ward, and Brianna was brought in shortly after. I spent the day in a fog, introducing baby Brianna to more friends and family. I still felt extremely weak. The doctors kept a close eye on my blood count, and by the afternoon, they recommended I get a transfusion. I wasn't improving. All day my visitors had commented on how pale I was. My mom said I looked "white as a sheet." Erv and I were both nervous about me getting a transfusion. Did the benefits outweigh the risks? Was this really necessary? Erv's blood is type O, making him a universal donor. We investigated the option of Erv giving me his own blood. We were told that was not an option. As the hours passed, my condition only grew worse. We finally decided to get the blood transfusion. Erv said goodbye to me for the night as they began giving me a stranger's blood. Almost immediately, I was feeling better. My energy returned, and I was anxious to go home the next morning.

At 8 a.m., Erv picked me up from the hospital with a brand new air conditioner sticking out awkwardly from the trunk of our car. "I guess I'm not going to surprise you when we get home," Erv joked. "Here's your baby gift." On this hot, sticky day at the end of June, that air conditioner was a beautiful sight to behold! It was an extravagant gift that I knew was costly for Erv to give. When we got home, there was also a beautiful bouquet of roses picked from our garden on the dining room table. It was surrounded by scribbled "pictures" drawn by big sister Mikayla. I sat on the couch with my baby girls while Erv installed the shiny, new air conditioner. I had so much to be thankful for.

Tent for Four

When Brianna was just 4 weeks old, we ventured out on our first camping after the girls were born. We were excited to introduce our baby girls to one of our favorite activities. Our destination was Old Orchard Beach in Maine, the same place where we had gotten engaged five years earlier. We would be meeting up with some dear friends from Oneonta, Julianne and Russ. They were fellow campers and parents of 6 month old Ethan. I was nervous about camping with babies, but I had done my research. I read that newborns were great to camp with. They slept most of the time, and when awake, they were not mobile, so they were easy to manage. Since Brianna was nursing, we would not need to pack bottles or special food for her. Her Pack-n-Play (inherited from Mikayla) fit in our new tent (bought on clearance as an anniversary gift to each other). The way we had raised Mikayla thus far, she was used to sleeping anywhere. We brought my old sleeping bag from my girl scouting days (literally 20 years earlier) and figured she would be just fine.

Erv and I prefer to travel light. As I packed up our car for the four day outing, I was conscious to bring as little as possible. Mikayla was just beginning to talk and didn't give me much feedback on packing. To save space, I left her big, bulky teddy bear (cleverly named "Bear") home in favor of a smaller, stuffed blue horse she had enjoyed as an infant. Once we got to the campsite, 300 miles from home, she asked for Bear. Then she cried for Bear. Then she screamed for Bear. We had been at the campsite for five minutes. I was in big trouble.

"You didn't pack Bear? Her bear that she sleeps with every night! What were you thinking?" Erv asked, frustrated.

"I was thinking we've got four people, two car sets, three sleeping bags, a tent, a cooler, and a Pack-n-Play in our car, and I wanted to save space. I'm sorry." I felt terrible and foolish for making this critical error.

Not able to run home and grab Mikayla's precious teddy bear, we went into problem solving mode. We headed to the on-site camp store to see if they sold any stuffed animals. They didn't. I tried to comfort her with the little, stuffed blue horse. It didn't work. That's when I spotted the playground. We brought Mikayla to the swings, and she was quickly distracted from thinking about her teddy bear. Crisis averted - at least until bedtime.

Our friends met up with us in the late afternoon, and we enjoyed dinner cooked over our camp stove. Mikayla was covered with dirt from head to toe after playing on the ground while the adults visited. Baby Bria and our friends' baby Ethan sat side-by-side in their car seats under my long bridal veil, doubling as a mosquito net. I cleaned up Mikayla the best I could with baby wipes, and we put all three kids to bed. The babies fell asleep quickly in their Pack-n-Plays. Mikayla was a different story. As the adults sat around the campfire sipping hot cocoa, Mikayla started whining, "I want Bear. Can't sleep without Bear!" Not wanting the babies to wake up, Erv went quickly into our tent to settle Mikayla. He never came back out. When I snuck into our dark tent to check on them a few minutes later, my Girl Scout sleeping bag was empty, and Mikayla was sound asleep on Erv's chest.

Erv was half-asleep and encouraged me to go back out and enjoy our friends. After an hour of chatting around the fire, I rejoined my little family in our tent for the night. I had just fallen asleep when Brianna started to cry. Not wanting to wake up the whole campground, I quickly lifted her out of the Pack-n-Play and started to nurse her. Or at least I tried to. She was not interested. Instead of nursing peacefully in the dark, she fussed and cried. Mikayla and Erv startled awake, and I quickly left the tent. Her cries seemed only magnified by the dark openness of the forest surrounding us. I tried walking with her, bouncing her, rocking her in my arms. She continued to cry. Her cries echoed off the rocks and trees. It was the loudest crying I had ever heard. We were surrounded by tents full of sleeping families. I needed to do something and fast. I suddenly spotted temporary salvation. Our 1988 Reliant K car. At least in there, the crying would be muffled. I slipped into the backseat and shut the door.

Once seated inside, I tried again to nurse Brianna again. She fussed and cried but eventually settled down. I'm sure it helped that I was finally relaxed, not worried about waking the world in the middle of the night. As Brianna nursed, I dozed sitting up in the car. I was so tired after a long day of driving and a stressful afternoon fretting over Mikayla's teddy bear. I longed to sleep stretched out in my sleeping bag. Brianna started to fuss once more and then full-out cry. Not again, I thought. At least this time, we were confined to the car. We stayed there all night. Brianna would cry, nurse, settle down and then cry again. This pattern continued all night long. I was thankful to pass her off to Erv in the morning. Our second night was a repeat performance. Brianna and I both spent the night in the car. By the second morning, we cut our trip short and headed for home. I don't recommend camping with babies.

The next summer, we tried it again. I had spent a busy year doing campus ministry with two babies. Our hand-me-down double stroller made the rounds across campus. Erv was quite busy between work, taking classes, being a teaching assistant, and studying for qualifying exams. Once the stress of those challenging tests passed, he began research for his dissertation. He suddenly realized why most people quit their Ph.D. programs during this phase. During that year he also switched jobs again, from working at the county to assisting a financial planner. The new position gave him more flexibility, allowing him to teach part-time and giving him more experience in his field. By the end of the jam-packed school year, we were anxious to get away to our favorite escape - the outdoors.

After experiencing our Maine camping fiasco along with us, our friends Russ and Julianne suggested a different destination. We joined them at a family camp in the Adirondacks. We wouldn't be as far from home, and this facility had a host of programs to accommodate families. There were sing-a-longs and rodeos and rafting trips. It sounded like an ideal place for us all to enjoy ourselves. The price was a bit higher than we would typically pay for camping, but it was still much cheaper than a hotel vacation. Brianna had been sleeping through the night for months, and Mikayla's bear was safely packed in the car. We were confident that this would be a successful family camping trip. We left in our crowded little car with high hopes.

This is one of many occasions where Erv and I learned the importance of reading the fine print. There were many unique adventure opportunities offered at the camp. Unfortunately, they all required an additional fee. Erv and I were forced to decide which one activity we would pay for out of the five we had selected when we chose to come to this camp. While the children were quite content with playground swings and ice cream cones, Erv and I were disappointed. We were excited to go white water rafting, horseback riding, and repelling. These activities were the whole reason we'd chosen this campground. It was tempting to go with the original plan and do everything we wanted. Technically, we had the money to do all the activities we wished. But we had a goal. We were saving to one day purchase our own business. If we didn't say no to tempting opportunities now, we would not be able to say yes to better opportunities later. We made the choice to live without our immediate want in of our future desires. This had been our philosophy for years, and it had served our family well.

Lazy and No Fun

It's amazing how the stress from home follows you and only becomes magnified when you travel. I don't think this is true for all people. For some, travel is a wonderful escape from the reality waiting at home. Erv and I are not especially good at separating ourselves from reality. While we made financial progress throughout the year, our relationship had suffered. It felt like Erv was always gone or busy studying. I was juggling working and taking care of two little ones, while also cooking and cleaning our home. We both felt there was more to do than either of us had the time for. There were days I would get resentful and make a list of all of the things I had done throughout the day, seeking to prove to Erv that I was harder working than he was. He would then make his own list of everything he had done all day, and it was just as long as mine. We both fought off resentment and struggled to put ourselves in each other's shoes. This family camping trip was meant to be a break from the busy schedules and long days apart. It seemed that goal was slipping away.

Making yet another financial sacrifice while on vacation caused a darkness to settle over our campsite. Erv was moody and distant.

I was on eggshells, not wanting to increase the disappointment. Erv retreated to the tent to take a nap. I struggled to keep the girls occupied while trying to cook our dinner. Mikayla was not yet 3 years old and mildly helpful. She could fetch plates from the car or ketchup from the cooler, but she was more interested in stacking rocks into interesting formations on the ground than she was in helping me make supper. Bria had just turned 1 and was learning to walk. She would totter around the campsite, using the tent poles and picnic benches to steady herself. She was basically a walking train wreck. Her preferred direction of movement, however, was up. In just 10 minutes, she had managed to climb up onto the picnic table, scatter the paper plates, and dump out all of the Kool-Aid. As she scooted across the table toward the camp stove, I yelled to Erv for help. I needed a second set of hands before a true disaster broke out!

Still groggy from his nap, Erv stumbled out of the tent. He picked Brianna up from the table and placed her on the ground by Mikayla and her pile of rocks. "Play with your sister," he said, and he grabbed a book and settled into a lawn chair by the campfire. Mikayla swiftly placed herself between Brianna and the precious pile of rocks, not wanting her baby sister to ruin her elaborate creation.

"No Bri Bri! No!" Mikayla scolded. Brianna was trying to reach the priceless rocks. I could tell Mikayla was ready to swat at her.

"Mikayla. Keep your hands to yourself!" I corrected. Though it'd be best to physically put some space between the girls and give Brianna something different to play with, I already had a big mess to clean up, and I didn't want to leave the camp stove unattended. "Share with your sister." I was doubtful this would work, but I hoped so. What I was really hoping was that Erv would get involved in this situation. He continued reading his book.

I started cleaning up the Kool-Aid and the spaghetti pot boiled over, putting out the fire on the camp stove. Brianna reached for another rock, and Mikayla screamed. As I struggled to get the stove relit, I asked Erv, "Aren't you going to help me?" My resentment from the many days spent juggling babies while preparing dinner as Erv studied in the living room back home came flooding over me. "You are so lazy!" I complained. Erv stood up and walked toward me. He kept right on walking, right out of the campsite.

Words spoken in anger rarely get us where we want to go. I managed to relight the camp stove, feed the girls dinner, and put them to bed. When Erv came back, he was hurt. "How could you call me lazy," he asked me, baffled and insulted. "I work two jobs while going to school full time. I never go out to dinner or out for drinks with the other students after class. I always come right home so I can help you. You are always on edge, worried that I'm going to be upset at anything you say. You walk on eggshells all the time and you're not even fun anymore."

Now I was hurt. Not fun? Me, not fun?! Who could he possibly be talking about? If I were to make a list of my defining characteristics, I would put "fun" near the top! I love to have fun, and I enjoy making ordinary activities fun for other people. This was the ultimate insult. But as we sat in silence staring at the campfire, I knew he was right. I had become paranoid about making him angry. The stress of school and work and small children running around was a lot for Erv. I was always trying to insulate him from it. I had stopped speaking my mind, making silly suggestions, and going out of my way to infuse our lives with humor and creativity. I wasn't as fun, and I was the one getting angry. I wouldn't ask for help, but I would be angry when I didn't get it. What started as a bitter argument slowly evolved into a frank and helpful discussion.

Our commitment not to go to bed angry proved helpful once again as we talked into the wee hours of the night. We certainly didn't resolve everything in a few hours, but we had been honest with one another and were making progress. Erv committed to help out more. I committed to ask for help more and worry less. And I would be intentional about being more fun. By morning, we were looking forward to our one big excursion on this camping trip. It was timed perfectly after our difficult evening. We had signed up for a trail ride and rodeo. The girls got to ride in a hay wagon with our friend Julianne and little Ethan while Russ, Erv, and I rode on horseback. It was a beautiful, relaxing tour through the Adirondack wilderness. After our ride, we enjoyed the playground while waiting for the rodeo to begin. Our girls were thrilled when the horses came galloping through the starting gate. We spent the next hour admiring and enjoying the colorful display of courage and talent. By the end of our camping week, Erv was very helpful with the girls, and I was extremely and undeniably fun.

Built-in Car Seats

Of the many things we learned on our camping trip, one of the less exciting discoveries was that we needed a new car. Our wedding gift used K car was more than decade old. We had been paying for small repairs for years, and more little things kept breaking. The right-hand passenger's side door had a broken latch, which we eventually had to tie shut to keep it from swinging open when making a right hand turn. Whenever I was the passenger, I had to enter on the drivers' side and then scoot across the bench seat. This was after loading two girls into their car seats, one on either side of the car. I was always exhausted by the time I actually got to sit down.

With our busy schedules and Erv's new job across town, we really needed a second car. Our friends Evelyn and Mark had recently bought a new car, and they generously gave their old car to us. It was an old sports car with high mileage and only two doors. We enjoyed the luxury of having a second car, although we didn't enjoy paying double for gas and insurance. Erv loved that it was sporty, but it was extremely difficult to get the car seats into. With the K cars in the shop more frequently, the four of us would have to pile into the little sports car. And then the sports car started making funny noises and had an interesting smell. We were waiting to get the K car back from the shop so we could put the sports car in when we got the doomsday call. The engine block was cracked. Unless we wanted to put a new engine in our very old car, we were out of options. We started looking for a new car.

When I say new, that's not really what I mean. We are personally highly opposed to buying new cars. The value of a new car drops dramatically the moment you drive it out of the parking lot. New cars cannot hold their value. We are also personally opposed to car payments. We believe that car payments should be made to you, not a dealership. Car replacement was one of our budget categories, along with other auto related expenses like gas, insurance, and repairs. We knew that our car would not last forever, and we had been putting money away each month for a "new" one. Using this plan, our money was earning interest at the bank instead of us paying with interest at the car dealership. We had saved up enough to buy an inexpensive car for cash.

I was more than happy to buy a used car. We never had a new car growing up, and I did not feel like we needed one. But I did not want just any car. We had two small children, and I was hoping to one day have more. (I still did have a uterus after all.) I also was regularly stuffing college students into our little car. I wanted a mini-van. This was my dream vehicle. Not only did it have more seating, it had more storage for the stroller, Pack –n-Play, portable high chair, and other baby-related paraphernalia. It also had more room for camping gear - a serious issue on our last two outings.

Erv was morally opposed to my plan. He hated mini-vans. I believe this is a common male opinion. He believed there was nothing masculine about a mini-van. To him, it felt like selling-out. He was already a married father of two in his twenties. Most of his friends were still single and driving new Saturns. He was not going to live like a middle aged suburbanite, driving around town in a boxy mini-van. That would not happen. I actually believed him.

We came to a compromise. We began looking for a Ford Escort station wagon. This would give us more storage space, but it wasn't a mini-van. Erv could live with that. I still wanted the extra seating, but I was supportive of this decision. I began searching ads in the local auto sales magazine and called every car dealership in the Albany area. I spent hours making phone calls, doing the research. I created a whole comparison chart outlining the year, mileage, and special features of each available car. We picked the five that fit our budget and seemed like the best deals. We drove to each individual seller or car dealership and test drove them all. We haggled with each seller to get a quote of their best price. Then, we'd make the rounds again, trying to get them to out bid their competitors. We had it down to two cars when we stopped at a random dealership alongside the road.

I couldn't believe Erv was stopping. It was a small dealership with only five or six cars for sale. All mini-vans. Not an Escort station wagon in sight. As Erv walked me up to the dark grey Dodge Caravan, my eyes lit up like Christmas trees. Not only was this van a good deal with relatively low mileage (meaning less than 100,000 by our definition), it had something I had never seen before. Something that I knew would make our lives so much easier. Something I never knew I wanted until I saw it with my very own eyes - built-in car seats. They were located in the second row. They hid away inside the regular seat and then easily flipped down to become regular child seats. There were many times when I would have to take our car seats out of the K car to have room for our college students on the way to an event or to church. With these seats, I wouldn't have to move anything when I had a Campus Ambassadors event. These built-in seats were glorious!

Unfortunately, they were too expensive. Even when we talked the dealer down, this van was $1,000 outside of our price range. We could not buy it. We would not finance it. We would live without it. But we could not bring ourselves to buy anything else. The Ford Escort station wagon we had chosen just could not live up to those built-in car seats. And now that Erv was open to a mini-van, I was not satisfied with a station wagon. We prayed and asked God for the mini-van. We knew we couldn't afford it, but we refused to give up hope. We went back to the dealer. He really liked us and the girls and wanted to help, but this was his rock bottom price.

The summer was coming to an end, and we went on one more weekend camping trip with some friends from church. Amy and Jamie were also young parents, their baby Annie was just months younger than Brianna. We shared with them about our disappointment over the mini-van with the built-in car seats. They listened and were empathetic. While on our trip Erv and Jamie went swimming in the nearby river. The current was fast, and they could literally body surf their way downstream with the rushing water. They made several trips down the river before climbing out to join us for dinner, but as Jamie came out of the water, he realized his watch was missing. This wasn't just any watch. This was his father's very special college graduation present. A Rolex. His father had called it a "man's watch," and it was a precious gift to Jamie. Erv and Jamie began diving, searching the river bottom for the watch. The current was moving so fast, it was impossible to see. All they could do was feel their way along the rocks at the bottom. Amy joined in the search, and I stayed with three small girls alongside the river, praying that they could accomplish the impossible. They searched and searched for almost an hour. I started to think this was pointless and thought maybe they should give up.

I had no idea how much a Rolex watch costs. I would buy a new watch every few years when the leather band would wear out on mine, and I usually paid $10, maybe $20 for a new one. Erv knew better. Though he did not know the exact cost, he knew this was a valuable gift to Jamie, and he was determined to keep looking. The three of them were just about to give up when Amy miraculously came up with the watch in her hand. It was amazing! I couldn't believe it. I had seriously given up hope. That watch could have been anywhere down there. How did she find it?!

Jamie and Amy were very grateful that we were so supportive of searching for this treasure. While Erv wasn't the one who actually found the watch, his persistence and dedication kept them motivated to look until it was found. As we sat around the campfire that night, we learned the watch wasn't just a special gift to Jamie because it was from his dad- it was worth more than $1,000! They were so grateful, they offered us the $1,000 we needed to buy our "new" mini-van. Complete with built-in car seats.

Erv's Bottom Line

* None of us know how long we have. If you have kids, get life insurance, and a will. Know who you would want to raise your kids.

* When your wife gives birth – she gets a gift. Everyone else will fawn over the baby; you fawn over her.

* Camping is an inexpensive bonding vacation. But bring the kids special nighttime comforts, and if you have babies -good luck.

* Bridal veils make great mosquito netting.

* Read the fine print.

* If you want something in the future it will require sacrifice today.

* We all say stupid things in our anger. Best to hold your tongue whenever possible (literally if necessary) and apologize when you don't. And use the opportunity to communicate something important that needs to be addressed.

Chapter Ten:

Tightwad Travelers

Trip for Two

After two summers of family vacation, Erv decided it was time for just the two of us to get away. We had kept to our weekly "date nights" pretty well, but our "lazy, no fun" breakdown in the Adirondacks showed us that we needed some quality time together. Raising two little ones just 20 months apart was rewarding but also stressful and demanding. A friend once told me that during this stage of parenting, "The days are long, but the years are short." We were finding this to be very true and we were thankful for these precious girls; however, time to focus on each other was needed. We started looking at childcare options. My mom loved the girls, but she was dealing with health issues. Caring for the two of them at once was too much for her to handle. Erv's mom had moved to South Carolina. She would have loved caring for them, but we would need to bring the girls to her. While a southern vacation sounded nice, that wasn't exactly what we had in mind.

Erv and I had always dreamed of international travel. When I was young, I remember staying with a neighbor who had just visited Israel. It sounded fascinating. How exciting to walk the steps of Jesus! Erv had always longed to visit China. He was intrigued by Asian culture and wanted to experience it first-hand. We had even considered becoming missionaries to China when we were first married. When we met with our church mission board about our vision, they encouraged us to try a short-term mission trip instead. They thought a year in China would be a challenging first experience overseas. Shortly after that conversation, I became pregnant with Mikayla, and the idea was abandoned altogether.

Israel and China were still way outside of our price range, but a different and interesting opportunity opened up to us. The University at Albany was home to many international students. Several of these students became involved in Campus Ambassadors, and I enjoyed the multi-cultural environment they provided for our group. Unable to travel the world, it was wonderful to see God bring the world to us through our international students. They would take turns cooking us traditional meals. We learned various cultural forms of worship and (best of all) they invited us to visit them once they returned to their home countries. One of these students was Victoria, an exchange student from England. After spending a year with us on campus, she had returned home and welcomed us to stay with her family in Oxford. We thought that England was an ideal place to start our international travel, considering they spoke English. My heritage is primarily British, which added interest for me as well. We would be provided with free food and housing so our primary expense would be plane fare. We had managed to save up enough over the past few years to purchase two plane tickets (if we got a good deal). This seemed like the perfect opportunity- but what about the girls?

When I mentioned this trip option on the phone to my friend Pam, she insisted that we pursue it. "You have a free place to stay for 10 days in England?! It's your sixth anniversary, you have to go."

"Yes, but we don't have anyone to take care of the girls. We've tried several options and nothing seems to be working out. Maybe we aren't meant to go," I responded.

"Then I'll watch them!" I couldn't believe what I was hearing. I had asked our parents, but I hadn't even considered asking friends. Taking care of a 2 year old and a 3 year old at the same time? It seemed like too much to ask anyone. Plus, Pam and her husband Mike already had three small children of their own. They would be caring for five children, all under the age of five!

"Are you serious?" I asked.

"Yes. Of course!" Besides the obvious insanity of asking my friend to care for five small children, another problem was that Mike and Pam lived in Chicago - a 12 hour drive from Albany. "No problem," my friend explained. "You guys can drive out here, spend a few days with us, and then fly out from Chicago. We'll keep the girls while you're in England, and then you can fly back here. We can visit a few more days, and then you can drive home. When are you coming?"

It was too good to be true! Our friends in Chicago were making a huge sacrifice so we could make our dream come true of taking an international trip. Meanwhile, Victoria's family was willing to let strangers stay in their home and eat their food all because we ministered to their daughter while she was in a foreign country. With all of these factors coming into perfect alignment, we made plans to celebrate our sixth anniversary overseas - something I would have considered impossible on our wedding day.

Planes, Trains, and Automobiles

Anyone considering a trip to Europe expects it to be expensive. Our trip certainly could have been if it weren't for Victoria's family and their generosity toward us. And yet, there were several other factors that were within our control to keep our expenses low. The first was purchasing our plane tickets. We didn't work with a travel agent but instead put in bids at a variety of Internet travel sites. We found that if your dates are flexible, you can save hundreds of dollars per international ticket. We knew we wanted to be in England for our anniversary, but other than that, our dates were open. We flew coach, and we didn't check any bags. It felt wonderful to pack everything we needed into two small suitcases that fit in the overhead bin.

After lugging bulky baby supplies everywhere, we felt incredibly free. Packing this light does require a bit of planning (and perhaps wearing some of your clothes more than once), but it makes traveling more convenient and affordable.

Once in country, whenever we weren't traveling along with Victoria's family in their car, we used public transportation. We were staying in Oxford but took a bus into London for a day. While there, we purchased another ticket for an all-day "hop on, hop off, double-decker bus tour." This allowed us to travel all over the city, seeing the sights for one inclusive price. We visited beautiful cathedrals, bridges, and museums. We only went inside a building if it was free to enter - and many of them were. We enjoyed wandering through the corridors, admiring the extraordinary architecture. I was especially excited to visit St. Paul's cathedral. It was 6 pounds each to enter, so we opted to enjoy our bagged lunch on the majestic steps out front instead. After lunch, we fed the pigeons our leftovers just like the "bird lady" in Mary Poppins. This felt like "experiencing" St. Paul's to us! Our one splurge of the day was a visit to the Tower of London. We enjoyed this tour but spent most of the time evaluating if it was worth the 12 pounds each. Not very impressed with the crown jewels or the ancient torture chambers, we decided we had overspent on this tour. Our experience in general with tourist attractions is that they over promise and under deliver.

In Oxford, the next day we signed up for a free walking tour. We enjoyed learning the history of the city while strolling through the colleges, streets, and gardens. That evening we paid 10 pounds each to watch a performance of Macbeth outdoors in one of the college courtyards. The ticket price included a cup of mulled cider, and the performance under the stars was absolutely magical. If you ever visit Oxford in the summer, we highly recommend a courtyard play (with genuine British accents). We spent the next day, our anniversary, in Oxford again. We meandered through the quaint shops on the main street looking to make a small purchase commemorating our visit. While browsing through a tea shop, I secretly smiled as I heard Pachabel's "Canon in D" playing. This was our wedding march, and it was playing on our anniversary! When I pointed this out to

Erv, he directed me to look out the window. I thought the music was coming through the store's speaker system, but it was actually coming from outside. We hurried out of the shop to find a string quartet playing our wedding march right in the street. As we moved closer to enjoy the beautiful live music, Erv wrapped his arms around me. In dream-like fashion, the musicians began walking in circles around us as they played the familiar melody. This was the perfect anniversary gift. Instead of an overpriced trinket, God had provided us with a priceless memory. All the trouble we went through to get away, just the two of us, had definitely been worth it.

On our final day in Oxford, Victoria invited us to enjoy one of her favorite English past times - punting. We rented boats for a small fee at one of the University colleges along the river Chawell. We each took turns standing at the stern of the boat, a long, heavy pole in our hands. We would use the long pole to push off the bottom of the river and propel the boat forward. This looks very easy, and the other boaters going by seemed to be effortlessly moving forward. I could not wait to try it. I immediately sent us crashing into the left river bank, then the right river bank, and then back into the left. It seemed impossible to keep the boat moving straight ahead. Fortunately, my turn was short. Erv took over and managed to keep us moving straight ahead. We stopped at a pub along the riverside called "The Victorian Arms." The pub lawn rolled right up to the river, and it was littered with college students relaxing in the midday sun. We docked our boat and enjoyed a late lunch before heading back up the river. It was a beautiful day of new experiences and inexpensive fun.

After five days of enjoying Oxford, Bath, and the Cotswolds with Victoria and her family, it was time to venture out on our own. We had purchased discount tickets for the train (by European standards we were still "student age"), and we headed north. We love traveling by train. Not only is it economical, it's a wonderful way to see the countryside. The views are magnificent, and you meet some pretty interesting people. The European rail system runs like clockwork so it's very reliable.

Our first stop was in the fabled town of York. We only had a few hours to visit, so we decided to tour the town from the top of the city walls. York has more miles of intact walls than any other city in England, and we wanted to capitalize on this unique experience. We pretended to be armed soldiers protecting our territory as we peered out of the arrow slits in the walls- it was great fun. We felt like a couple of rebellious college students on summer vacation.

Next we walked along "The Shambles," a famed narrow street where the upper levels of the buildings jut out and almost touch each other. It was on this street that we spied "Ye Olde Starr Inne." Since the place was named after us, we decided it was the ideal spot to enjoy lunch. We were tempted to buy a replica sign from our namesake establishment but decided against it. We had two more cities left to visit, and we needed to be careful with our remaining spending money. I had already purchased a beautiful pair of silver earrings. A pair of inexpensive earrings are my favorite souvenir because I'll actually use them, and am reminded of my travels every time I wear them. We also bought a Beanie Baby Bear with the Union Jack on it for the girls. Beanie Babies were all the rage in 1999, and we thought this would be a special treasure for the girls.

We took a tour of the York Cathedral, which was every bit as impressive looking as St. Paul's in London, except this tour was free! We also climbed up to the Multangular tower. Or at least I did. After walking all over the city, Erv was tired out and chose to wait in the gift shop while I climbed the 45 steps to the top. The view from this ancient battlement was spectacular and well worth the effort. Erv assured me afterwards that he would enjoy my pictures upon our return home. Time had passed quickly, and we hurried to the train stop. We looked forward to our evening destination - Berwick-Upon-Tweed.

Berwick-Upon-Tweed was recommended to us by one of my fellow Campus Ambassadors employees, Joel. His wife is British, and they had spent extensive time traveling around England. He thought Erv and I would enjoy this charming coastal town along the border of England and Scotland. The city was surrounded by Elizabethan walls. While it was still daylight, we explored the little city and the beautiful coastline. It was cold and windy, but Erv was especially excited to see the ocean. We even spotted a few seals playing in the water. We stopped at a little pub along a side street and paid less than 10 pounds for both of us to eat supper, our only expense that evening.

We spent the night in a charming little bed and breakfast, our favorite place to stay outside of a tent. Our housing cost included a traditional Northumberland breakfast, which was huge. I could barely finish my meal of eggs, ham, biscuits, and other things I could not identify and was afraid to ask about. The next day we toured Berwick Castle and Lindisfarne Monastery. This was a special place as the monastery was founded by St. Aiden, the first missionary to bring Christianity to England. The following day, we took the train up to Edinburgh, Scotland. As soon as we came out of the station, bagpipe music filled the air. The stonework of the buildings in Scotland was distinctively darker than in England. It was a foggy, rainy day, but that didn't stop us from enjoying our tour of Edinburgh Castle. We found it more impressive than the Tower of London, and the entrance fee was half the price. At the end of the day, we took our last train ride up to Glasgow where we would catch our plane in the morning. We stayed at another bed and breakfast in a little town called Lochwinnoch, just outside of the city. It had a beautiful garden where we relaxed and reflected on our memorable journey. By now we were both worn out and ready to get home to our girls.

The girls had a wonderful time with Pam and Mike's family. I was a little sad when I heard Bria accidentally call Pam "Mama" upon my return, but little Bria quickly assured me that she indeed knew who I was. We spent a few more days all together enjoying each other's sweet company in Chicago before the long drive back to Albany. Once again the kindness of friends and the faithfulness of God had made the impossible possible.

Erv's Bottom Line

- ✶ Days can be long, but years are short.
- ✶ You can really experience and enjoy a new place on a limited budget.

- ✖ Love to be generous – especially to your love. And accept the generosity of others who love you.
- ✖ I highly recommend punting if you visit England.
- ✖ When traveling, mix in with the locals if you have the chance.
- ✖ Prices of attractions don't always add up to what you get. It tells you more about the number of visitors who will go to that location. Take time to get off "the beaten path."
- ✖ You can easily save money having two meals while traveling. A late morning meal and an early dinner, and still have opportunity to enjoy the tastes of the region.

Chapter Eleven:

Five Starr Family

Dr. Starr on the Horizon

Erv was finally able to see the light at the end of the Ph.D. tunnel. He had passed all of his qualifying exams, finished his coursework, and was wrapping up his dissertation research. He began applying for positions at Christian colleges teaching business. His very first interview was at a Baptist college in the mid-west. I was not excited about moving so far away, but Erv was determined to teach at a faith-based institution. He wanted to be able to include biblical principles in his teaching. That choice meant we were definitely leaving Albany, a truth that did not sit well with me. We had lived in Albany for five years now, and it had become our home. We had a wonderful church, close friends, and family nearby. We were established and comfortable. But Erv had worked hard earning his degree, and I did not want my comfort to stand in the way of his dreams. I emotionally prepared for our family to move.

Erv was not offered the job in the mid-west, and I felt a sense of relief. I knew it was only a matter of time, but for now I celebrated our temporary stability. The girls were getting bigger, and both of them finally graduated out of diapers. It was a monumental event which was five years in the making! We were enjoying our growing girls immensely, and they blessed us with their smiles and funny antics every day. The four of us were relaxing with some friends on the front porch when we heard some very sad news. One of the families in our youth group had lost their oldest son. He had been struck by a car while crossing the road and did not survive. It was a tragic loss, and their youngest son was left an only child.

We couldn't help but think how difficult this would be for the younger brother. To be left all alone after years of companionship. It made us think of our girls. They were very close and did everything together. We couldn't imagine if something happened to one of them, especially once they were teenagers. The loss to us as parents would be great, but we imagined it would be even greater for one of them to be left all alone. When we were first married, we had wanted a big family- at least three or four children. When the girls came so quickly and so close together, we had put that idea on hold. Was it now time to have another child? We had never planned a pregnancy before so this felt a little strange. We gave the idea of having a third child some serious thought for about five minutes. That's all it took. I was instantly pregnant.

Erv continued to look for teaching positions throughout the school year. I cringed as he sent applications all across America. I really did not want to be a plane ride away from family, especially now that we were having another baby. I wanted this child to know his or her extended family. Annual visits at Christmas or summer vacation would not be sufficient. Everyone was so excited about this expected child. Some hoped it would be a boy and yet most assumed we would have another girl (we were good at making those.) I had told Erv before that I would be willing to have a third child only if he could be excited about three girls. He assured me that he would be. The girls were very excited about their sibling-to-be. My growing belly was regularly rubbed and poked and hugged. Mikayla and Brianna attended "sibling" classes at the local hospital, learning how to properly hold, change, and feed the arriving baby. Erv's father was very attached to the girls and looked forward to our newest addition.

"You're going to miss Carrie and the girls and that new baby when you move," he would tell Erv, "because I'm not letting them leave. They're staying here with me." I was tempted to take him up on this threat.

When I heard that a teaching position had become available at Roberts Wesleyan College in Rochester, N.Y., I was elated. This was the opportunity I had been waiting for. Albany was only a four hour drive from Rochester and a five hour drive from my hometown. We could still visit family, and they in turn could visit us. We would be able to stay in touch with our friends and church family as well. I didn't know much about the school or the community, but this job became my first choice. Erv had a friend from his Ph.D. program who had been teaching at Roberts in the same department, and he really liked it. We were both hopeful that God would open this door for us.

Delivery Room Reject

The upcoming year flew by quickly as we prepared for several transitions. Because we were definitely moving at some point, I needed to make plans for the Campus Ambassadors ministry at the University of Albany. I was so excited when my friend Kim accepted the invitation to move to Albany. She would spend the year training with me and then would take over the ministry, providing a smooth transition from my leadership to hers when I moved. She would also provide me with a maternity leave (something I didn't bother to take after having Brianna). We loved working together and enjoyed collaborating on plans and ideas for the school year. We had a common vision for campus ministry and often said that we "shared a brain" making us able to anticipate each others' thoughts. Kim moved into one of the downstairs apartments at our house, became an integral part of our family. She would help me care for the girls and was a weekly guest at our dinner table. She joined us in our excitement about the new baby soon to come.

My pregnancy quickly progressed and my belly grew to an enormous size. Apparently, my body easily returned to its stretched out state the third time around. Kim commented that I was, "as big as a house," and my own mother called me a "cow." Before you take offense at my mom, you should know that she was only responding to me saying I felt like a cow but it still felt weird to hear her call me one! When my contractions started, I called my mom. As tradition would have it, she immediately came to town. Due to a decrease in her health, she was no longer driving but had received a ride from a friend (a generous offer since she still lived two hours away). She could only stay the night so we hoped the baby wouldn't be as slow arriving as the girls had been. We took the girls to Erv's brother's house and headed to the hospital with Mom. Four hours later, they sent us back home. I wasn't making any progress. They said it must be false labor. This was embarrassing. I had been in labor twice before, surely I knew what it felt like. Apparently, I didn't. By the next day, I still wasn't in labor. Mom had to leave town with her friend and without a grandbaby. I felt terrible.

A week later, the contractions came back. Mom decided she would wait a while before coming to town this time around. It wasn't easy for her to get a ride, and she didn't want to take any chances. It's a good thing she didn't. I was sent home from the hospital a second time. Now this was really embarrassing. You would think it was my very first trip to the maternity ward. How could I get it wrong, again? I was officially a delivery room reject.

As I went home embarrassed and disappointed, the contractions continued- for a week. They would increase in frequency and intensity (meaning pain!), and then would slowly decrease. They never disappeared altogether. As soon as I would start to relax, they would increase again. It became difficult to sleep. It became difficult to work. It became difficult to move. I was tempted over and over again to go back to the hospital, but I was determined to wait until I was absolutely sure I was really in labor. The day before our third child was due, my contractions started to increase in intensity, for the 400th time. They started coming faster and faster, but I would not go to the hospital. I would not be sent home a third time. They got closer and closer together, and Erv started to worry. He brought the girls to his brother's house, just in case. I still would not go to the hospital. "The next time I go to the hospital, I'm not leaving without a baby," I insisted. Erv headed to the car (which was full of gas, by the way). I stayed on the couch. What if I was wrong and I wasn't really in labor? I had to be sure. Erv honked the horn. I tried to stand up and ended up on the floor. I was in a lot of pain. I didn't know if I could walk. "I think I'm really in labor," I said to absolutely no one.

Erv came in the door. "We need to get you to the hospital. Now!"

When we arrived at the delivery room, I was thrilled to hear the doctor announce that I was truly and genuinely in labor. This time, I would not be leaving the hospital without a baby! When we came to the hospital on "failed attempt #1," we had been given the same delivery room where both Mikayla and Brianna had both been born. It was very exciting to think that all three of my children would be born in the exact same place. After "failed attempt #1," they wouldn't even give me a delivery room for "failed attempt #2." They simply put me in an observation room so I wouldn't waste anyone's time. Maybe I had been labeled a "faker." When they saw me come in the door for "attempt #3" unable to even walk, they offered me a delivery room right away. I asked for the very special "Mikayla and Brianna were both born here" room, but someone else was using *my* room! Instead of the large, pale green room at the end of the hall, we were given a small Pepto-Bismol pink room near the nurses' station.

This was humorous to us because our ultrasound indicated that this child was likely a boy. Of course, we didn't totally believe them after the "don't paint" experience with Brianna's ultrasound, but we were hopeful to be adding a boy to the Starr family. Being born in a bright pink room wouldn't be the most masculine entrance into the world. We did, however, manage to pass the time in a fairly guy-honoring way. It was game one of the World Series - the Subway Series - Yankees v. Mets. With Erv a Mets fan and me a Yankees fan, it was an interesting dynamic. We had the game on in our delivery room, and we would catch glimpses of the action between contractions. Because I was the one actually giving birth, the medical staff all sided with me. The Yankees came out on top, and our little boy came out right on time - our only child to be born on his due date. To this day, our son Connor is obsessed with being prompt.

Erv, baby Connor, and I spent the night in a private room on the maternity ward. We decided it was worth spending a little extra for a private room since I would be going home to mother three small children soon enough. I needed to get my rest while I could. We had heard a rumor that you were rarely charged extra for the private room, even though the hospital advertised the additional cost. We didn't put much stock in this rumor and had saved for the extra expense, but graciously, the hospital never charged us for the room. First thing in the morning, the big sisters came to visit their baby brother. Mikayla and Brianna climbed up onto the hospital bed with Connor and me, admiring their long awaited sibling. He was hugged and kissed and held and almost squished to death. They were instantly in love with this handsome young man.

Two days later, we all brought Connor home from the hospital. We weren't home five minutes when the phone rang. It was the Chair of the Business Department at Roberts Wesleyan College. He wanted to schedule Erv for an interview. This was an even better "baby gift" than the air conditioner I received the day I came home with Brianna.

House Hunters: Take Two

About a month passed, and Erv and I took a road trip to Rochester with baby Connor. While Erv was interviewing, I traveled around to the different college campuses in the area seeking a place to start a new Campus Ambassadors ministry if we were to move there. It was the first weekend of December, and all the little towns were decorated for Christmas. The different communities looked inviting, and the College at Brockport struck me as the perfect place to start a new ministry. We enjoyed meeting the Chair of the Division of Business and his wife, as well as the other faculty and staff at the college, and easily pictured ourselves living in this new community. We drove home hopeful that this place would become our future.

A few days later, Erv was offered the job! We started to make moving plans. Now that I had seen where we were headed, I was no longer worried but excited about this next chapter of our lives. The timing could not be more perfect as the two bedroom apartment that seemed so large when we first moved in, now seemed small and crowded. The girls had grown out of their cribs into bunk beds, and Connor was sleeping in a cradle in our bedroom. The small apartment was not made for a family of five. The postage stamp backyard had no room to run, and our street was too busy for Mikayla to learn to ride a bike in. I was so excited to start looking on the Internet for our new home!

I wanted to live in a house. A real house. Not an apartment. I found a beautiful house for sale right across from the campus. It had four bedrooms, two bathrooms, a lovely front porch, a yard with a pool. It was perfect. Erv, however, found something else. It was also near campus, had four bedrooms, two bathrooms, and a yard. But this house had something more. Something that made him very excited. It had a two car attached garage with an apartment above it. - an apartment we could rent out to help pay for our new mortgage. After collecting rent for four years, Erv was committed to multi-family housing. I was open to the idea, although I liked my house option a lot better than his. Unfortunately, both houses went off the market before we could even talk to a realtor. Again, our timing was terrible.

Two months later, we made a trip to Rochester for the weekend to meet with a realtor and look at houses in person. We were shocked at the mortgage we qualified for with Erv's new salary. This dollar amount was higher than we expected and made us face yet another temptation. If we bought a house at the maximum amount we qualified for, the high mortgage payments would make us feel constantly strapped for money. We had been strapped for money for years. We had worked hard (especially Erv on his PhD) so that we didn't have to be tight on cash all the time. Why would we put ourselves back in the same position just to have a bigger house than we really needed?

We found a beautiful, old colonial house just a few miles from campus that we both fell in love with. It had four bedrooms and two bathrooms (our minimum requirements), but it also had a swimming pool, a beautiful front porch, a gorgeous fireplace, and most importantly, land that backed up to a creek where we could go canoeing. It was a real temptation. Erv's mom and stepfather had given us a canoe for Christmas, and unfortunately, it didn't get much use. Strapping it to the top of our van and driving it somewhere after loading up three kids rarely happened. If we bought this house, we could leave our canoe by the creek side and use it whenever we wanted to! The house was available for private sale, so we made the family a verbal offer, taking $10,000 off their asking price. They were thrilled.

Once the offer was made, Erv couldn't sleep. This house was at least $20,000 more than he planned on paying or could pay for comfortably. Even though it was technically less than we could afford according to the mortgage company, the monthly payments would mean squeezing every other area of our budget. There would be no wiggle room, and that made us both uncomfortable. We were sick to our stomachs and cancelled the deal two days later. Back at our apartment, we were disappointed. Our house hunting trip to Rochester had been a waste, and we were right back where we had started. Discouraged, we tried looking on the Internet again. Erv could not believe his eyes. The original house he had chosen months earlier was back on the market - and with a reduced price!

We headed to Rochester for another round of house hunting, this time with all three children in tow. By now we had seen lots of homes with fireplaces, dishwashers, and large yards. They had generous square footage and charming features. We couldn't bring ourselves to pay for any of them. They just didn't seem to be worth the money. Surely we could find what we wanted for a more reasonable price. It was already May, and we were hoping to move at the end of June. We needed to find something this time around. It was on this third fateful trip when we met our ultimate temptation.

Our realtor showed us yet another beautiful colonial with a front porch, large bedrooms, fireplace, and a brand new $30,000 kitchen.

It was stunningly, amazingly gorgeous! I love kitchens. It's where I spend the majority of my time at home. The brand new cherry cupboards went up straight up to the ceiling. The granite counters glistened in the sunlight as we made our way across the ceramic tile floor. There was a charming desk/work station right there in the kitchen. It would allow me to keep up with my ministry email and paperwork while making dinner and entertaining children. There was a breakfast bar where the three kids could enjoy an afterschool snack while they did their homework. I could picture our whole family enjoying this kitchen. It only had three bedrooms, but with the kitchen desk, I wouldn't need an office. The girls could keep sharing a room, and it would be fine. We wanted that kitchen.

Before we could make any final decisions we needed to visit Erv's Internet find with the apartment over the garage. It wasn't available to show until the afternoon. I was fixated on that kitchen at the other house. Visiting this garage apartment house was simply a formality. Erv felt like it was not a coincidence that his house, complete with rental income, had come back on the market. He would not make an offer on the amazing kitchen house until he saw the garage apartment house. Brianna and baby Connor fell asleep in the realtor's car on the way across town, and I decided to let them stay in the car and rest while we looked at the house. Everyone wanted the amazing kitchen house, so they didn't really need to see this one. I expected us to be back in the car shortly.

We rang the doorbell of the white, Cape Cod style house. We entered the brown paneled breezeway and walked through the small, carpeted kitchen. The homeowner offered 5year old Mikayla some Doritos, which she happily ate sitting at the kitchen table. Meanwhile, Erv and I investigated the rest of the house. It indeed didn't take long. There were two small bedrooms and a bathroom on the first floor, and a good sized living room with a large picture window. Upstairs were two large bedrooms with lots of shelves and closet space as well as another full bathroom. I was intrigued. This house had much more space than it looked like from the outside. Then the realtor took us to the greatly anticipated garage apartment. It had a large, open kitchen, dining, living combination room, a separate bedroom, and a full bathroom. It was clean and bright and surprisingly spacious.

The realtor took us outside. There was a large backyard with a row of tall pine trees along the back, giving the illusion of being in the woods instead of suburbia. Then we were brought to another back yard, behind the pine trees. This house came with a double lot. From this yard, you could see to the Roberts' campus. The realtor pointed out a brick building about 100 feet away. It was Carpenter Hall, the home of Erv's future office. That got our attention. Walking to work would mean we could go back to one car and cut our automobile budget almost in half. This house became more and more interesting to us both.

This house didn't have a $30,000 kitchen, a fireplace, or even a dishwasher. The other house had all of the above. We were torn. Did we go with the economical choice as we had for the past seven years of our marriage - the smaller house with rental income and walking-to-work, one-car option? Or did we enjoy Erv's new income and buy the beautiful house with the brand new kitchen of our dreams? We decided to make an offer on the amazing kitchen house. We had worked hard. Erv finally had a real income. We deserved a $30,000 kitchen.

Once the offer was made, we both felt sick. It was too expensive. We didn't need a $30,000 kitchen. We had made the same mistake again. It was not a wise choice. We should have chosen the smaller house with the rental income and the option to walk to work. We had allowed our emotions to cloud our better judgment. We tried to stay excited about our beautiful new kitchen, but we both knew it wasn't worth the cost.

Fortunately, our offer at the amazing kitchen house was rejected by the seller. They wanted more money. They were hoping we would counter with a higher price, but we didn't. We both breathed a sigh of relief and asked our realtor to write an offer for the garage apartment house. It was $20,000 less than the other house, and this house provided income from the apartment. Erv asked his dad if he would help put in a fireplace and asked his step-father if he would help put in a dishwasher. Both said yes and our economical dream home was born!

Erv's Bottom Line

* A planned pregnancy is great. So is a big family. I give it a 5 Starr rating.

* Just because you have had a baby, doesn't mean you know what to expect the next go round.

* Don't take life for granted – embrace each day.

* False labor is like the feeling we get when we think a new "thing" will make us content/happy. We soon realize it won't "deliver."

* Waiting for something wonderful is worth it and builds anticipation. This is true for a new member of the family or saving to buy something special.

* Dave Ramsey's quote, "If you live like no one else, later, you can LIVE LIKE ONE ELSE" is true over time. We aren't there, but we are seeing our lifestyle improve.

* Just because you qualify for something (e.g. a large mortgage) doesn't mean it is wise to take a loan that large.

* Living close to work has many advantages. From low car costs, to home lunches, and the convenience of retrieving forgotten work items.

* Left to ourselves we often make the impulse emotional decision. Later, with perspective, we think differently. Give yourself time to gain perspective.

* Anytime someone pressures us to make a decision NOW, we have a standard answer: NO (it has served us well).

* You can make changes to a home, but it is difficult to change its location.

Chapter Twelve:

New Horizons

Free Family Fun

We spent the first night at our new home lighting sparklers on the front porch steps. Nine month old Connor sat in my lap as he held the bright, shiny sparkler, his hand wrapped securely inside mine. Brianna had just turned four years old and happily ran circles around the Mountain Ash tree in our new front yard. Five-year-old Mikayla chased behind her, laughing with joy. Mikayla was probably the most excited about our new home. When we first arrived at the house that morning, she charged through the door with a disposable camera in her hand. She ran into every room taking pictures. She snapped photos of every window, every door, and inside every closet. "This place is a mansion!" she exclaimed. "I never thought we'd live in a mansion!"

Erv's younger brother, Jason, and his wife, Heather, made the journey to Rochester and helped us get settled into our new home. Saying goodbye to them was the hardest part of our move. Erv's brother had lived in the apartment downstairs from us for two years. Once Jason got married to Heather, my childhood best-friend, they moved into an apartment just blocks away. Heather had cared for our children during Campus Ambassadors' meetings every week for five years while we were in Albany. She and Jason were always willing to watch the children and were the primary reason we never paid for a babysitter. They were very disappointed about our move. They even considered looking for jobs in Rochester so they could live near us. We all cried as we watched their car head back to Albany the next day. This was going to be harder than I thought.

Our first few weeks in Rochester were quiet and surprisingly peaceful. It was strange to have days go by without the phone ringing. We felt a little bit like we were on a vacation. Living in this new home didn't seem like reality. The house felt mammoth (all 1,500 square feet of it!) after being squished in a two-bedroom apartment. The girls happily shared the large upstairs bedroom. For the first time, we had space to put both of their beds right on the floor. After years of bunk beds, this was exciting! There was also plenty of space for dance parties and fashion shows. Connor had his own spacious room, also, right across the hall from his sisters. Erv and I were happy to have a bedroom to ourselves once again. It was about time for our "little roommate" to move out. Having an "adult" bathroom and a separate "kids" bathroom was glorious! Three expansive yards (almost a full acre of land) and a quiet neighborhood where the kids could safely play were a delight. All that scrimping and saving so we could one day buy this house was feeling very worthwhile.

I would wake up early each morning with Connor and roller blade around our new neighborhood, pushing him in the stroller. He would squeal and laugh as we spun around the corners. This was our special time together and an energizing way to start the day. My new neighbors got to know me as the "rollerblading baby lady." Once we returned home, everyone was awake, and we'd plan the day's adventures. We found many free or inexpensive outings for families around Rochester like several beautiful parks and playgrounds and a free beach along Lake Ontario that even had concerts open to the public every Wednesday night. We signed the girls up for discount swim lessons at the college and purchased an annual membership to the local children's museum. For the same cost as two family visits without membership, we could go to this wonderful museum as often as we'd like all year long. Our family would visit at least once a month, making it well worth the investment. We purchased a membership to the city zoo with the same philosophy. The zoo has a fantastic stream where the kids could cool off by playing in the water between excursions to various animal habitats. In the summer, we visited the museum and the zoo almost weekly, getting our money's worth within the first month. For the rest of the year, it was free!

While enjoying lots of family fun, we also got to work making our new house into our dream home. The house had two front doors - both bright pink. I hate pink. It is my least favorite color in the world. I have changed my favorite color about seven times in my life, and it has never, ever been pink. No house of mine was going to have pink doors. Not a chance. I purchased a quart-sized can of colonial blue paint (my current favorite color), and the pink doors were gone by day two of our residency.

As if pink doors weren't hideous enough, there was also carpet in our new kitchen! Who puts carpet in a kitchen? I could not understand it. When you have three small children, food gets spilled in the kitchen a lot. It's basically a daily occurrence. Cleaning sticky food off a carpeted kitchen floor is a completely unpleasant experience. But carpeting in the kitchen had forced this home to be sold at a bargain price, so I didn't complain. I ripped it out. Of course Erv and his handyman dad helped me. We took the carpet out of the kitchen and the breezeway entry. We laid ceramic tile, found for $1 a square foot in the clearance room of the local home repair store. Because the tile was a discontinued line, there were limited quantities of each color available. There wasn't enough of any one color to cover the floor. Our solution was to buy two different colors and lay them in a checkerboard pattern. The finished product looked great - far better than carpet - for minimal cost with our own labor. We were already increasing the value of our home. I was happy.

We also painted the dark wood paneling of the breezeway, installed a gas insert fireplace, and added a chair rail. What was once a dark, chilly entranceway had now become a cozy, inviting family room - my favorite room in the house. Discovering that the hardwood floors of the living room extended into the dining room, we pulled up that carpet, as well. This was much more difficult than the kitchen. The carpet had been glued right to the hard wood floor! We had to melt each square inch with an iron and scrape the carpet and glue off the wood with a putty knife. It took hours and lots of patience. We then hired one of the maintenance workers from the campus to refinish our hardwood floors. We tried to do most jobs ourselves, but we were tentative about this one. This wasn't what our new friend did professionally, but he had just finished the gym floor at the college. He was comfortable with the job and gave us a discount price. The newly refinished floors turned out great. The house was transforming, making it more enjoyable to live in. We were so glad we didn't overpay for a house in perfect condition. It was much cheaper to transform our discount house into the home we wanted.

Erv's famous garage apartment totally lived up to our expectations. While the moving truck was still in our driveway, two different young couples from Roberts came to our door. They both heard we had an apartment and wanted to rent it. We never even advertised and had our choice of tenants! We enjoyed getting to know the lovely young couple we selected and found it to be a pleasure sharing our living space with them. We also appreciated the rental income contributing to our new mortgage payment. For our first year in Rochester, we chose to retain ownership of our apartment house in Albany, as well. Our friend, Kim, lived in the house and collected the rent for us. The additional income allowed us to purchase our home with a 15-year mortgage. This meant higher monthly payments but much lower interest paid over the life of the loan. This mortgage was later refinanced to a 10-year mortgage at an even lower interest rate. Most people considered this impossible, but we had gotten so used to living on less, we didn't mind the higher mortgage payment and avoiding having to pay 30 years of interest!

As our family income grew, we were determined to use the extra money for giving, as opposed to more spending. From the beginning of our marriage, we had been committed to giving a percentage of our income to the Lord's work. When our income increased, we tried to increase that percentage. We went from sponsoring the

Compassion International child Erv had "adopted" in college to sponsoring four children from various parts of the world. We were excited to financially support our campus minister from Oneonta and continued adding others to our missionary family. As more of our dreams were starting to be realized, it was always a temptation to limit our giving. The checks written out to our church were growing, as were the missionary donations. We continued to look at our budget, ensuring that we were being generous with the income with which God had blessed us.

Hungry in Hungary

Erv was enjoying his new full-time teaching position at Roberts, and I found starting a new Campus Ambassadors ministry at Brockport rewarding. Mikayla began kindergarten at the local public school while Brianna and Connor continued going to work with me. Erv walking to work was a real benefit as he would come home for lunch every day, allowing him to connect with both me and the children. It also meant an inexpensive, homemade lunch. Mikayla's half-day program at school meant we could continue our free trips to the zoo, parks, and children's museum throughout the school year on my days off.

We officially celebrated Erv's graduation with his Ph.D. in December. Mikayla was not happy to ruin her perfect attendance record in kindergarten but missed a day of school to attend the ceremony. I found myself unexpectedly emotional as I sat in the bleachers. This degree was a formidable mountain to climb, and it had taken its toll on all of us. I was extremely proud of Erv and personally thankful to have survived. I would no longer hear Erv say, "I'm not here. I have homework to do," as he sat on the living room couch at night. Now when the kids went to bed at night, we would finally have time for each other. That is, until I decided I had plans of my own.

Campus Ambassadors requires their staff to receive a seminary education. I always agreed with this policy on a philosophical level. However, with five years of working part-time in ministry and full-time as a mother of preschoolers, it hadn't exactly fit into my schedule. I was regularly asking for extensions to postpone my seminary education. Now that Erv was finally finished with school, it was my turn to be a graduate student. With Erv working at Roberts, I could attend Northeastern Seminary at the college for free. Classes were held one night a week, specifically designed for people juggling school with work and family. It was a perfect fit for me.

Erv and I were blessed to meet many new students on our respective campuses. I was excited to begin my ministry by working with international students at Brockport. After enjoying the rich diversity at the University at Albany, I was glad to meet students from around the world at this new campus. Erv had a special affinity for international students as well and connected with one in particular on his campus named Russell. Holding duel-citizenship in Canada and Hungary, Russell brought a rich perspective to the classroom. Erv and Russell began reading books together on economics (the focus of Erv's undergraduate degree) and met weekly on campus for a time of discussion and mentoring. By the second semester, Russell invited us to visit him in Hungary the following summer. He also wanted to introduce us to some missionaries using business concepts to provide jobs for the poor in Romania.

Erv thought the idea of learning more about business and missions work in Hungary and Romania sounded very exciting. When Erv suggested we go there with Russell, I was tentative. Actually, I was terrified. Russell was going to be with us for the first half of our trip, but we would spend the second half on our own. We didn't speak Hungarian or Romanian. I loved the idea of assisting missionaries and seeing new places, but this was a little scary to me. Most short-term mission trips I knew of were done with a group, not a couple who had never been to that country before. When God provided free childcare for us once again, I had no excuse.

Erv did some research online and found a great price on tickets. Russell used his hometown connections and missionary contacts to find us inexpensive housing in both countries. We arrived in Budapest with our carry-on luggage in tow. It's a good thing we pack light because Russell gave us a tour of the city by foot. We dragged our rolling luggage across the cobblestone streets, alongside the Danube River, and up to the Parliament building. After touring Heroes Square, we headed by train to Russell's home city of Gyor. The train was absolutely packed. We had to sit on our luggage in the aisle. When we arrived in Gyor, we found a charming little town with a center square lined with cafes and shops - a common stop for German tourists. Russell took us to a small inn where we would spend our first few nights. We had a tiny little room with slanted ceilings. If you sat up quickly in bed, you would smack your head hard. We learned this from experience.

Russell returned home to spend the night with his dad, and Erv and I were left to fend for ourselves for dinner. After a long day traveling, I was starving. I am blessed with a crazy high metabolism, so I am used to eating about every two hours. It had been almost 20 hours, and I was dying for some food. We chose a small restaurant just a few blocks from the inn. We were nervous about ordering on our own without Russell to help us. It turned out to be an exciting adventure. We both pointed to something on the menu and anxiously waited for our selected meals to arrive. We found drinks to be the easiest to order in both Hungary and Romania. Fortunately, a Coke is "Coke" all over the world.

Our time in Hungary felt more like a honeymoon than a mission trip. We enjoyed strolling around the beautiful town, eating delicious food, and having long uninterrupted conversations. I don't think Russell knew it, but this was exactly the trip we needed. The longer we were married, the more obvious it had become that marriage takes intentional work. Experiencing new places together gave us fresh conversation starters and infused our familiar relationship with new energy. Our second night, after Russell had gone home, Erv and I ate out at Café Mozart, a charming outdoor café complete with wrought iron tables and chairs with blue umbrellas and white tablecloths. I felt like I was a character in a romantic movie. The prices for food in Hungary and Romania were incredible. Most of our meals on this trip were eaten out, and we paid an average of $4 each per meal. I would not have thought to travel to Hungary for a romantic vacation, but we found it to be perfectly lovely and pleasantly priced.

On the fourth day of our trip, Russell brought us to the train station to see us off to Romania. I did not want to leave. Not only was I disappointed to vacate this beautiful place, I was scared to leave Russell. He had been our guide thus far, speaking the language and showing us the way to go. Now we would need to navigate on our own and somehow communicate what we needed. I pushed back my fear and confidently stepped into our rail car. We spent all day on the train from Gyor to Arad, Romania. It was hot and smoky, and it seemed we would never arrive. When we finally pulled into the station, my anxiety returned. The moment of truth. We needed to find our way to the home of Russell's missionary friends.

I'm still not quite sure how we got there, but we managed to find the house. I was very excited to meet these kind American women serving the Lord in Romania. Later that evening, they brought us to meet another missionary friend named Lee. Lee was from England, and he had an intriguing ministry to street children. He was providing housing and jobs for teens without homes. The boys he worked with ran a variety of businesses. Some worked the farm where they all lived. They raised pigs and vegetables. Others were selling bicycles made from closeout parts donated to the ministry. Still others were running a bridal shop where they rented out wedding gowns. Lee found all kinds of creative ways to employ young adults instead of seeing them live in the streets. He was very inspiring. After spending another day touring Lee's various businesses, we packed up our bags and got back on the train. It was another long ride from Arad to Sighisoara. The views were beautiful as we arrived in the Transylvanian mountains.

In Sighisoara, we met two more American missionaries, Dorothy and Elizabeth. Dorothy had lived in Romania for several years and owned her own home. We stayed with Dorothy in a little apartment on the top floor of her house. From our window, we could look out over the red clay tile roofs of the other houses in the city. We spent the next day playing with young children in the "family center," a part of the ministry where they served food and provided educational activities for those in need. The following day was the most challenging of our trip. We visited a hospital for abandoned children. We volunteered with our new missionary friends, holding babies and playing with toddlers who had no families to visit them. We had been given nursing scrubs at the front desk in the hospital lobby and were instructed to put them over our clothes. We were told we could take any of the babies out of their cribs to hold them as long as we had the scrubs on. Having a baby of my own at home, it was heartbreaking to see row after row of cribs full of babies, with not a single adult in sight. We passed three rooms full of babies and still hadn't seen anyone caring for these precious children. As we made our way from room to room, holding the babies, I had to resist the urge to sneak one home with me.

Our last day in Romania was my birthday. We visited yet another ministry for underprivileged teens. Dorothy was using a similar model to Lee, using small businesses to help fund the needs of children whose families could not afford to care for them. One of their businesses was giving guided tours of the Citadel. Erv and I took a tour of the beautiful city, admiring the architecture, and enjoying the folklore. At the end of our tour, we treated our guide to dinner at a local restaurant. We were shocked to learn that she had never eaten there before because it was too expensive. Our dinners were only $3 each. That was a real eye-opener for us about the reality of poverty around the world. An extremely cheap dinner out for us was an extravagance to this young lady.

That evening we took one last, long train ride to Bucharest. We exited the train at 1 a.m. As we made our way from the outdoor platform to the station, several men came up on both sides of us, seeming to want to carry our baggage. We had been told not to accept any such offers. We'd been warned of the high crime rates at the train station and tried our best to ignore their menacing insistence to help. We searched for a legitimate taxi driver, complete with certification papers, and asked for a ride to the International Airport. We took turns sleeping uncomfortably in the airport, waiting for our morning flight to Rochester.

The 12 Month Couch

We arrived back home with a newfound appreciation for all that we had and a vision for helping ministries through business opportunities. This was the beginning of our passion for social entrepreneurship, using business to solve social problems instead of simply making a profit. Erv would soon put this model to work as he entered a new business partnership with his cousin, Chris. Together Erv and Chris bought a rent-to-own store. This business had been established as a means to make furniture and appliances available to the poor by providing low monthly payments. The problem with this model was the interest charged through the payment plans. The customers would end up paying three times what the item was worth by the time they own it. Erv and his cousin phased out this old model and instead promoted a "90 days same as cash payment plan," still making the merchandise more accessible to the poor without taking them for granted with interest payments. They held workshops for their customers, providing personal finance advice, including the benefit of the "90 days same as cash" program.

Erv enjoyed partnering and teaching with his cousin in this business. Although the business was actually located back in the Albany area, where Chris lived, he made visits to the company and spoke frequently to Chris on the phone. This new venture allowed him to bring real life experience into the classroom. He felt good to be employing sound business principles and celebrated achieving his dream of having his own business. The added income allowed us to give more and support other ministries. It also allowed us to save more for future business opportunities that would multiply our efforts to help others.

Even though we were thankful for the increased income, we continued to live frugally in all areas possible. We had become accustomed to living below our means, and we desired to stay there. We were thrilled to discover an Aldi grocery store and a dollar theatre in Rochester. We shopped for our children and ourselves, at the Salvation Army thrift store. I continued cutting everyone's hair at home, and garage sales were our department stores. We ate peanut butter and jelly sandwiches every day. I would rinse out our plastic baggies and reuse them. When we did make big purchases, we made them carefully, taking our time to find the best deal.

Now that we were living hours away from our friends and family in Albany, we frequently had weekend visitors. We loved having company, but we lacked a comfortable place for them to stay. After saving up the money, we decided it was time to purchase a living room set, including a sofa bed. Since the furniture store we owned was four hours away, we headed to the local discount store to purchase our new furniture. I was so excited at the very thought of picking out something new for our family. I had grown up with hand-me-downs my whole life, and we had been living with hand-me-down furniture for almost 10 years. As we looked at the various couches and chairs in the large showroom, one set in particular stood out to us. It was blue and white plaid, with big, loose pillows along the back. It came with a sofa bed, love seat, lounge chair, and ottoman. It was perfect. It was priced reasonably, too. We sat on it. We laid on it. We tried to keep the children from jumping on it. Everyone in the family loved it. We left the store.

After the "creek side property house" and the "$30,000 kitchen house," we had learned to take our time spending big chunks of money. It was easy to be emotional in the moment and make an impulse purchase. We needed to go home and think about it. If we really wanted the furniture, it would still be there tomorrow. We visited two more stores and went home empty handed. Over the course of the next 12 months, we went back to that store 10 more times. Every time, we would go sit on that couch, and then look at all the other couches. And then we would leave. When we were finally convinced that this was indeed the living room set we wanted to buy, we paid for it with cash and opting to purchase just the couch and loveseat. The added time helped us conclude that we didn't really need the chair and ottoman. As much as we liked them, they wouldn't have fit well in the living room, and we saved money. It was the greatest feeling in the world. No sleepless nights worrying. No sick to our stomach feelings that we had overspent. Our friends thought we were crazy taking 12 months to decide on purchasing a living room set. If they thought that was crazy, they would not believe what we would do next!

Erv's Bottom Line

* Seeing through the eyes of a child can make the ordinary extraordinary.

* Enjoy the seasons of being near family, they don't always last.

* Exercise with your baby – it's healthy, fun, and setting a good example.

* You have already paid for community parks, playgrounds, and recreational areas. Enjoy them.

* Memberships can pay for themselves rather quickly. This can be a great way to enjoy a special place all year long.

* Look at the bargain sales in any store you frequent. You can find really great deals.

* Keep your mortgage loan to 15 years (or less) if possible.

* You are blessed in order to bless others.

* Bring your lunch most days. You can still eat with friends and colleagues and save money.

* Traveling to "less expensive" countries is still fascinating, full of adventure - and easier on the purse.

* It's ok to wait for something you "really, really" want. Especially, when that means you can pay for it with cash.

Chapter Thirteen:

From Camping to Cruising

Fashion Show

We always knew we wanted to do something big for our 10th anniversary. We had been saving toward it since our visit to England four years earlier. Every month, we were consistent at putting away a little more money. Erv was the mastermind behind this plan. We were finishing our second year in Rochester, and Erv had a new co-worker in the business department at Roberts. Marcia had come from the corporate world and brought with her a wealth of experience. She and her husband had enjoyed extensive travel, and she served as an excellent getaway consultant. Of all the trips she and her husband had ever taken, her favorite was an Alaskan cruise. This was her strong recommendation.

Erv came home from work excited to share his idea for our big anniversary trip. I loved the idea of a cruise but had always imagined sunning myself on a pool deck, sipping a drink with an umbrella in it. The thought of bundling up with a wool blanket while looking at icebergs did not have the same appeal. But Erv was determined that this was the dream vacation we were looking for. A Caribbean cruise was common. An Alaskan cruise was an adventure!

We headed to the computer to do a little research. After discovering that an Alaskan cruise would allow us to take helicopter tours of glaciers, ride bikes in the Yukon, and mushing sled dogs through the snow, I decided that Marcia knew what she was talking about! Learning from our Adirondack camping trip, we made sure to read the fine print. Each of these excursions would cost extra, but we decided they were all "once in a lifetime" experiences. We carefully planned our itinerary according to the amount of money we had saved. We scheduled one special outing for each day we would be at port. The rest of the time, we would take advantage of the meals and entertainment included in the price on the ship. When choosing our cabin, we employed our family philosophy: the minimum plus one. We had decided that we minimally wanted an outside cabin so we could enjoy the view. We upgraded this one level and chose a room with a balcony. We avoided the temptation to upgrade to a suite, assuming that we wouldn't be using the room much anyway. We expected the private balcony to be a pleasant treat when we wanted to be outdoors but away from the crowd.

After making all of the arrangements, I realized we had additional expenses to consider. Neither of us had ever been on a cruise before. As we began sharing our excitement with friends, I was asked a common question: "What are you going to wear?"

"Warm clothes. It's Alaska," was my typical response.

"No, I mean to dinner?"

I didn't realize that you had to get dressed up for dinner on a cruise. I had only seen the people on cruises in commercials wearing bikinis. I knew I wouldn't be wearing one of those, but I didn't know I would be wearing fancy dresses. I did not own any fancy dresses. We are not the dress clothes type. Even though Erv wore a suit to work almost daily, I had never been to the dry cleaner. I use those special bags you can put in the dryer to clean a husband's suits. It's much cheaper. I, myself, didn't have much occasion for wearing dress clothes. I enjoyed being paid to wear jeans and T-shirts to work every day. This is a huge benefit to campus ministry.

I looked at my closet. I did have a growing collection of bridesmaid dresses. This seemed the perfect occasion to finally get my money's worth out of those. As I tried them on one by one, none of them seemed "cruise-like." They were distinctively bridesmaid-sy. I was in trouble. I looked at the cruise itinerary. There were three nights I needed to be dressed up. We would be seated at a table with the same people every night. I could not wear the same dress three times. I would need THREE nice dresses. This was ridiculous.

I got in the van, loaded the kids into the built-in car seats, and drove to my favorite Salvation Army store. They had a whole section of dress clothes. Surely they had something cruise-worthy. I filled my cart with every dress in my size, regardless of the style or color. I lined up the kids outside of my dressing room and the fashion show began. "Ooooo Mommy! You look pretty," Brianna would respond to every one. Mikayla would quietly shake her head "no." Since Mikayla is the source of my best fashion advice, I would return to my dressing room and try again. On dress #13 I got my first Mikayla head nod. It was a navy blue, tank style dress - simple, elegant, $7 plus tax. Sold!

We moved on to the Goodwill store. Having exhausted all of my options at the Salvation Army, I needed more inventory. "Carrie Cruise Wear Fashion Show, Take Two." Another cart full of fancy dresses. Another dressing room. Another line-up of small Starr children prepared to make their mommy look fabulous. More "oohs and ahhs" from Brianna. More head shaking from Mikayla. By now, Connor needed to be bribed with food just to sit still. Fortunately, my bag was stocked with granola bars, buying me time to try six more dresses. On dress #8, I got another head nod. And applause from Brianna. Connor joined in on the applause, and I felt slightly conspicuous. While my children sat on the floor happily clapping, I stood wearing a floor length black dress with a slit up the side. It had an open back with skinny horizontal straps going across. Purchase number two. $12.

I was out of granola bars for bribing Connor and out of patience. While most women enjoy shopping, I find it a completely unpleasant process. I decided that two dresses would suffice. On one of the fancy dinner nights, we would skip the formal dining room and opt for the midnight all-you-can-eat chocolate buffet. The thought made me wish I hadn't bought any dresses at all. Well, now that I had spent almost 20 bucks, I was definitely wearing them!

High Expectations

Because Erv's student, Russell, was also Canadian, he gave us some friendly traveling advice. He encouraged us to fly into Seattle and take a bus into Vancouver. This would be much cheaper than flying directly into Canada. We drove the kids four hours to Albany where they would spend the next week with Aunt Heather and Uncle Jason. The next morning, Jason drove us to the airport before dawn. We felt like typical tourists checking luggage. I didn't want to squish my fancy new dresses into a carry on, and Erv felt his suits would survive better in a garment bag, as well. I also wanted to make sure I had plenty of layers for our outdoor excursions. When we arrived in Seattle, we checked in with the bus company. We had plenty of time to get to Vancouver before our cruise set sail. We boarded the bus, excited to be one step closer to our exciting journey.

We soon discovered that something was wrong - very wrong. You know you should be scared when your bus driver begins looking at a map while driving, as ours was doing. He would pull into a parking lot and turn around. Then he would look at the map again. Then he would turn around again. Our confidence in him was waning. We looked at our watches. We had less than two hours until our cruise was scheduled to leave. The two hours became one hour. The one hour became 30 minutes. When we finally pulled up to the cruise terminal, it was empty. There was no one in line at the gate. We hurried up to the counter and presented our tickets. "Skip the check-in procedures. You need to go right to the dock. Your boat is about to launch!"

Erv and I took off running toward the boat. We sprinted down the dock, pulling our heavy luggage behind us. I was regretting the fancy dresses and warm layers. I should have stuck to our standard of carry-on luggage only. As our bags bounced behind us on the dock, the crew was preparing to pull up the gangway. We were the last passengers to board, and then the boat pulled away from land. That was more adventure than we bargained for.

We were so late getting on the ship that we had missed the safety briefing. When we received our cruise ID cards, we learned that Erv had not even been assigned a life boat. I was assigned boat 14. After watching "Titanic" too many times, I promised to share my life boat with Erv. You can never be too careful.

We skipped the champagne at the Bon Voyage party on deck and opted for cans of refreshing Sprite. We knew that the two biggest money makers on board were selling alcohol and gambling at the casino. Neither held much appeal to us, so we avoided incurring additional expenses. As we made our way to our cabin, we were stunned by the massive size of this ship. (We kept getting lost the first few days.) The ship felt like a floating city with multiple restaurants, theatres, and shops. We finally discovered our cabin, and it was perfect. The very first morning, we were sitting out on our little balcony enjoying our devotions and spotted a killer whale jumping in the water below. The ship followed along the whale's path for several minutes before changing course. It was an incredible sight to behold! We were so glad we had spent a little extra on the balcony room. In that one awesome moment, we considered the extra money well spent.

Each morning, we took advantage of the on-ship workout facilities. The treadmills faced out enormous windows looking out over the bow of the boat. As we ran, it felt like we were skimming across the water. Because all our meals were included, we indulged in three meals a day. Typically when we travel, we reduce our food costs by eating only two meals supplemented by snacks. We were enjoying three meals a day, plus snacks. It's a good thing we started each morning in the gym. The typical cruise patron gains a pound a day on board. We could easily see why!

We were so excited about our first stop in the capital city of Juneau. This was our dog sledding day, and we both expected it to be our favorite. It was cloudy as we exited the ship, but that didn't damper our spirits. We were going dog sledding in Alaska, one of the coolest things on earth that two people could do! We walked to the designated terminal and donned our glacier boots. We would travel by helicopter over the Mendenhall glacier to the dog sled camp. This was going to be so incredible. It was like getting two trips in one. We were led to the helipad and climbed up into the chopper. Erv and I put on our headsets and gave each other a "thumbs-up."

We waited and waited to take off. Something was wrong. It started to rain. Then it started to pour. It was no longer safe to fly with the helicopter. Our tour was cancelled. We couldn't believe it. We exited the chopper and walked away dejected. We wandered aimlessly through the little tourist shops along the main street. It was totally and completely boring. We walked through the rain, disappointed at our luck. The highlight of our trip had become a dismal failure. We boarded the ship and pulled away from our favorite excursion opportunity. I was not excited to put on my fancy dress for dinner. We would comfort ourselves with all-you-can-eat ice cream instead.

The Most Expensive Day

There were two more stops along our trip. The next port was Skagway. It was the only other town along our route that even offered dog sledding and helicopter tours. We had already reserved (and paid for) a narrow rail Yukon train/bike tour that would occupy four hours of our day. The Skagway dogsled tours were all sold out. Erv refused to give up hope. When we docked at 6 a.m., Erv was the first person off the ship. He knew that the cruise ships worked in conjunction with local tour companies and decided to work with the tour company directly. I was still asleep in our cabin when Erv returned at 7 a.m. "It's raining and all of the morning helicopter tours are cancelled." This was not "good morning" news.

We went to the gym and breakfast, as usual, and disembarked for our train ride. At least this was not cancelled due to weather. We boarded the White Pass Yukon Route Railroad. The train ride through the majestic mountains was beautiful and the historic narration of the gold rush interesting. There was a small landing outdoors between each of the cars. I enjoyed standing out there, feeling the cool wind on my face. The air was so crisp and clear. It was still cloudy, but the rain had slowed down to a light drizzle. There was only one dogsled tour in the afternoon, but helicopter tours were scheduled for every hour. Maybe there was hope that we could take an afternoon helicopter ride. We tried to focus on the moment and take in the beauty around us. We chose to be thankful for what we could experience instead of what we couldn't.

When we reached Fraser, British Columbia, everyone taking the rail/bike tour exited the train. We were each given helmets and bright yellow windbreakers. The color was hideous, but it was good protection from the drizzle. Erv and I enjoyed speeding down the mountain on our borrowed bikes. Having been on several multi-day bike tours, we decided this was the way to handle big hills: take the train up and the bike down. We had crossed from Alaska into Canada while on the train up. On the way down, we got to bike across the border. It was fun to show our passports at the border patrol while on our bikes. The view along our ride was fantastic. We passed majestic waterfalls and steep mountain cliffs. Now we were really having fun!

By the time we got back to town, the weather had cleared, and we learned the helicopter tours were now running. Unfortunately, the tour company told us that every tour was sold out. We had missed our last chance to take a helicopter ride or a dog sled tour while in Alaska - the two things we were most excited about doing. Erv refused to take no for an answer. He left the tour office and set out on foot, heading straight out of town. I thought he was crazy. "I can see helicopters taking off and landing in the distance," he said. "That must be the airport. We're going there!"

I reluctantly followed my husband. This reminded me of our trek to the Colorado River at the Grand Canyon on our honeymoon. Ten years later and the same exact scenario. Once Erv had his mind set on something, there was no changing it. We walked for miles, heading further and further away from our ship and all our free food. I was hungry. I tried to convince Erv to turn around. He ignored me. "You can go back if you want to. I'm riding a helicopter." Of course, I kept following. We were celebrating our 10th anniversary. I wasn't very interested in hanging out on a cruise ship all by myself - even if they had incredible food in massive quantities.

Sure enough, Erv found the airport about four miles outside of town. We hadn't needed that morning workout after all since we power walked the entire way chasing helicopters. Erv walked up to the ticket counter. "All of our helicopter tours are sold out," the attendant told Erv. "Told you so" were my immediate thoughts. "But I can put you both on stand-by. If someone doesn't show up, you can have their spot." The dog sled camp was far up in the mountains. With the cloud cover, it was too dangerous to go, so the dog sled tour was cancelled. They were, however, still running helicopter glacier tours. I couldn't believe it. The door of possibility was open. It was only open a teeny, tiny crack, but it was open. We had already walked all this way. We decided we might as well wait and see if we could get on a flight. I raided the vending machine for a much needed bag of Skittles and grabbed an outdated magazine to pass the time.

We had waited for more than an hour when our names were called. A passenger on the next flight was more than 250 lbs. and wasn't willing to pay for two seats. If we were willing to buy two tickets, we could board the next flight. Although it had already been an expensive day with the train/bike tour, we decided it was worth it. We had planned on spending this much in Juneau and had gotten a refund. It wasn't a hard decision to purchase those two helicopter sightseeing tour tickets.

We put on glacier boots and boarded the helicopter. We donned our headphones and felt a strange sense of déjà vu. This time, we waited until the helicopter actually took off before giving each other the big thumbs up. The ground dropped away beneath us, and there was a sudden feeling of weightlessness. We climbed our way into the sky, following along a mountain ledge. As we reached the top of the mountain, it felt strange to keep on flying. The sensation was so similar to being on a roller coaster that I expected to go plunging back down to the ground. As we traveled along through the sky, we passed over several glaciers. The pilot identified the different formations, his commentary coming through our headsets. The incredible blue coloring reminded me of Superman's secret palace. It looked surprisingly delicious.

Halfway through our tour, we actually landed right on one of the glaciers. The pilot let us out so we could walk around. We explored the glacier and its giant crevasses. I was so tempted to jump across these giant cracks in the icefall. Considering each crevasse was at least three feet wide and hundreds of feet deep, Erv did not approve of my plan. He dragged me away from the death cracks, and we spent half an hour trekking around the glacier before re-boarding the helicopter. We took off and headed back to the heliport, enjoying incredible views of more glaciers and mountain ranges along the way. We absolutely loved our experience and found it well worth the cost. As we exited the chopper, we commented on how surprisingly easy it was to get a flight on standby. While leaving the heliport, we overheard someone comment that the dog sled camp had re-opened!

We rushed to the ticket counter. Had we heard correctly? Was the dog sled camp indeed back open? Could we get on a flight? "Sorry. The dog sled tours are all booked. You can try waiting on standby if you'd like." We waited. It had worked before. What were the chances of it working again? We at least had to try. This would be our ultimate Alaska experience, and it was our very last chance to make it happen. We waited and waited. This time I bought some Reese's Peanut Butter Cups and grabbed yesterday's newspaper. We could not believe it when our names were called! There were two seats open on the last trip to the dog sled camp. The trip was very expensive. We had already spent more money on this day than we had buying our living room furniture. It took us 12 months to decide to spend that money. We had 12 seconds. This single vacation day was going to end up costing more than our wedding day. We bought the tickets. It was a record spending day for the Starrs, but it had all been in cash that we had diligently saved. We both agreed that this collection of unique experiences was well worth the high cost.

We loved the second helicopter ride and decided that, one day, we want to own a helicopter. It was such an incredible feeling. We reached the dog sled camp and met our team. We were introduced to each dog by name. We petted each dog to greet them. They were so beautiful and friendly. We were given hats and gloves to fight off the extreme cold of the high mountains. After receiving instructions of how to command the dogs, we mounted our sleds. The wind whipped around us as the dogs pulled us across the frozen ground. Snow sprayed our faces. At first we went slowly, then picked up speed. I couldn't believe how fast the dogs could go pulling us behind them. Half-way through our ride, we stopped to give the team a rest. We both got off to pet each one and tell them what a great job they were doing. We took turns "mushing" on the way back to the camp. Fortunately, I was better at this than punting in England. Maybe I had found my calling. Someday, Erv and I will be giving helicopter/dog sled tours in Alaska. Before leaving the dog sled camp, we got to visit with some adorable sled dog puppies. It was a delightful end to an expensive and wildly satisfying day.

We spent the next day at sea, sailing through Glacier Bay. The decks were crowded, and we were glad to enjoy the view from our private balcony. As we sat huddled under a red, plaid blanket, I remembered my vision of this cruise when Erv first presented the idea. This was exactly what I had imagined - and it was perfect. The water was a bright bluish-green from the mineral deposits in the glacier. As we left the bay, we passed a brown bear and her cub on the shore - an incredible sight! In the evening, after dinner, we enjoyed a musical in the ship's theater. We had attended a different show every night, and we found them to be a delightful way to end each evening. We marveled at the incredible experiences we were having.

I was a little nervous about our actual anniversary. This was the one day we had selected an excursion that was not one of my top choices, but Erv was enthusiastically looking forward to it, and I didn't want to spoil his excitement. I would be a good sport and endure. I prepared myself to go snorkeling. Who goes snorkeling in Alaska? I am not a good swimmer. Erv assured me that the ¼ inch thick neoprene wetsuits would keep me afloat. I was concerned that they keep me warm. We neared the water's edge, and there were large chunks of ice floating in it. We had just passed massive glaciers in the water the day before. This seemed like a very stupid idea.

We were part of a group of 20 people, and each was given gloves and hoods to wear to keep us warm in the water. Once we began swimming, it was impossible to tell one person from the next. Everyone's faces were covered by the hood, goggles, or snorkels except for a small area around our mouths. I had no idea where Erv was. There were three guys with visible mustaches in the group, so I nonchalantly tried to follow them around, hoping one of them was Erv. Usually I could identify Erv by his unique height, but in the water, all the heads were at the same level. I would keep looking.

Once I got over my initial nervousness, I found my underwater exploration to be completely enjoyable. We saw beautiful jellyfish, sea urchins, salmon, and many other creatures that shall remain nameless. I even managed to pick the correct mustache guy at one point and was able to snorkel hand in hand with Erv. While it wasn't the anniversary experience I would have imagined, it turned out to be a wonderful way to celebrate our ten years of adventure together. Once we were out of the water, warm and dry, we toured the charming shops of Creek Street in Ketchikan. Erv surprised me by purchasing a simple, but beautiful, sapphire and diamond ring to commemorate the occasion. I'm not sure which I enjoyed more, the new ring or the saleslady thinking we must have married in elementary school to be celebrating our 10th anniversary.

As we sailed back to Vancouver, Erv and I reflected on our trip. It was hard to imagine that ten years ago, we started our journey together in a borrowed tent. Today we were standing on our private balcony on a cruise ship in Alaska watching dolphins play in the water below. We hadn't received an inheritance from a rich uncle. We hadn't won the lottery (neither of us had ever even purchased a ticket). We had simply made consistent choices to spend less than we made. We stuck to our values and pursued our shared mission together. We saved and invested in ourselves and in others. And now we were enjoying the precious reward of priceless time together.

I guess it pays to be cheap.

Erv's Bottom Line

- A great rule of thumb; "the minimum plus one." When you have a choice, pick what would be the minimum acceptable quality and then go one step up.

- You can buy used and still look amazing. Once you've worn something new one time, it's "used" anyway.

- Sometimes saving money adds adventure, too much adventure. But, what great stories they make after the fact…

- If you can travel in the "off season," you can get great deals.

- When in a new place or on a large ship – explore, wander, and see where your feet take you. There may be a wonderful treasure just around the next corner.

- Even the best laid plans can fall through. Love perseveres, hopes, and anticipates.

- It's ok to be persistent – and to ask even when things are "full."

- Sometimes you have to wait to get something worthwhile. It is worth the wait.

- You can splurge when you've saved for something diligently.

- Most of life's financial struggles or successes are the result of simple choices made over and over again.

- Marrying your best friend is a life adventure like no other.

Epilogue:
When Cheap is Hard

It's not always easy being cheap.

Sometimes you just want to spend money without thinking about it first. That's the reason to have a miscellaneous category in your budget. We all occasionally splurge on something. Just make sure it's occasional and record what you spend afterwards.

Sometimes people think you're cheap- because you are. This can be embarrassing. Don't let other's misuse of money define how you should use yours. Be as generous with others as you can within your budget and be at peace with your decisions.

When your pursuit of money overshadows your pursuit of God, be more generous. It's all His anyway. Give it away whenever you can. If you really need it, He can give you more.

It's easy to spend more money than you should on your kids. Don't succumb to the pressure of giving your children what everyone else has. Being cheap parents prevents having spoiled kids.

It can be hard to spend money when you've been cheap for so long. We sometimes have to remind ourselves that it's okay to buy things that we can afford.

We have friends who have told us they have, "beer pockets with champagne taste." It's hard to be cheap if you're accustomed to having expensive things. You can still have nice things. You simply need to save in advance for them and buy them less frequently.

It's tempting to be cheap with each other. Since we're both on the same page financially, it's easy for us to save by not spending on each other. We need to give ourselves permission to be generous when it comes to holidays and special occasions. If anyone in your family feels spoiled, it should be your spouse. Just check the budget to be sure you can afford it.

CPSIA information can be obtained at www.ICGtesting.com
Printed in the USA
LVOW041912291211

261628LV00001B/27/P